For UK order enquiries: please contact Bookpoint Ltd, 130 Milton Park, Abingdon, Oxon OX14 4SB. *Telephone*: +44 (0) 1235 827720. *Fax*: +44 (0) 1235 400454. Lines are open 09.00–17.00, Monday to Saturday, with a 24-hour message answering service. Details about our titles and how to order are available at www.hoddereducation.com

British Library Cataloguing in Publication Data: a catalogue record for this title is available from the British Library.

First published in UK 2011 by Hodder Education, part of Hachette UK, 338 Euston Road, London, NW1 3BH.

Copyright © 2011 Christine Wilding and Aileen Milne

Typeset by MPS Limited, a Macmillan Company.

Printed in Great Britain for Hodder Education, an Hachette UK Company, 338 Euston Road, London NW1 3BH, by CPI Cox & Wyman, Reading, Berkshire RG1 8EX.

The publisher has used its best endeavours to ensure that the URLs for external websites referred to in this book are correct and active at the time of going to press. However, the publisher and the author have no responsibility for the websites and can make no guarantee that a site will remain live or that the content will remain relevant, decent or appropriate.

Hachette UK's policy is to use papers that are natural, renewable and recyclable products and made from wood grown in sustainable forests. The logging and manufacturing processes are expected to conform to the environmental regulations of the country of origin.

Impression number   10 9 8 7 6 5 4 3 2 1

Year   2015 2014 2013 2012 2011

Contents

1   What is CBT?   2

2   Thoughts and moods   18

3   Adjusting your thinking   38

4   Additional CBT techniques   56

5   CBT and specific difficulties   70

6   CBT for developing strengths   84

    Conclusion   94

1

what is CBT?

The basic premise of CBT is summed up by the phrase: 'What we think decides how we feel.' CBT is a theoretical model that links our thoughts with our emotions and behaviour. It is a mix of cognitive theories and behavioural experiments, and is rich in techniques, strategies and applications.

Formulations are used to chart links between events, thoughts, emotions and behaviour. They are used to help clients to understand their thought processes and their effect. Events themselves don't cause us problems; it is the interpretation we give to an event or situation. The point of examining thoughts, feelings and actions is to build self-awareness.

In the initial stages, clients work with their therapist to define their problems, to identify what maintains the problems, and to establish the changes they would like to make. Short and longer term goals are set to provide markers along the way and an end point.

Cognitive behavioural therapy (CBT) is currently the 'buzz word' in therapy, but has been around since the 1960s. Aaron T. Beck and Albert Ellis were the prime innovators of what was then a new system of psychotherapy called *cognitive therapy*. Cognitive theories and techniques developed and were combined with behavioural experimentation methods leading to the birth of CBT. It was the first therapeutic approach to concentrate on thought processes and their connection with emotional, behavioural and physiological states. The concept that people could make choices about how they interpreted events in their lives was exciting and radical. CBT is centred on the idea that a person is capable of changing their cognitions and the effects of their thinking on their emotional well-being.

Its reputation and popularity have grown for a variety of reasons. Not only is it a clinically proven therapy applicable to a range of emotional problems but it also makes a process of change achievable in a short time, usually 6–20 sessions. It does this by breaking down self-defeating thoughts and beliefs, and by forming alternative life enhancing viewpoints. CBT has also proved its efficacy in brief therapy, which is usually completed in 4–6 sessions.

Scientific evidence shows that CBT is effective on its own or alongside medication. The therapist provides coaching in techniques and skills; which can then be practised independently, reducing the need for ongoing treatment which may be lengthy and expensive.

CBT is considered to be a practical, systematic and highly effective method of addressing an array of emotional and psychological problems. It has traditionally been offered by psychologists or psychotherapists, but has more recently become available through trained counsellors.

Strong structure and active participation is crucial to the success of the therapy. The kind of emotional problems helped by CBT include anxiety, depression, panic disorders, phobias, post-traumatic stress disorder, and obsessive compulsive disorder.

CBT addresses emotional and behavioural problems by drawing attention to thinking patterns and moods. When you are absorbed in emotional problems, you won't be at your most rational. You are likely to think in ways that further upset you. Negative emotions will escalate and your behaviour may become unhelpful, adding to the problem. As negativity builds, common sense and self-care disappear. You may 'catastrophize' and healthy thoughts may develop into self-defeating thoughts such as 'nobody loves or understands me' or 'I'm useless'. It's easy to see how this type of thinking becomes a vicious cycle of negative thoughts, emotions and behaviour.

A crucial CBT concept is that thought processes – thoughts about yourself, other people and life situations – have a huge effect on your emotional well-being. This is summed up by the statement: 'what we think is how we feel' or 'what we think decides how we feel'.

CBT proposes that when you replace self-denigrating thoughts with more realistic, self-accepting ones, positive changes will happen. The central aims of CBT are:
* to make you aware of your thought processes and their effects
* to enable you to make positive changes in your thoughts, beliefs and assumptions by enhancing your self-observational powers and self-reflective skills
* to increase your awareness of the effect of negative behaviours in the maintenance of your problems.

The development of CBT

The most famous pioneer

Possibly the best-known early pioneer of psychotherapy is Sigmund Freud (1856–1939). His psychoanalytical therapy emphasized the role of unresolved, unconscious conflicts from childhood as determinants of how we feel and behave. Freud believed that the way forward to emotional good health was for people to recall and make sense of their early childhood experiences.

In recent years, various experts have challenged Freud's theories, specifically pointing out that it was very hard to empirically prove their efficacy.

While many therapists continued to work with ideas developed by Freud, the 1950s saw the development of a psychology called 'behaviourism'. Based initially on work with animals, it purported that psychological problems were caused by faulty learning, and that most problems could be resolved by teaching people to change or modify their behaviours to achieve more positive results. In certain areas, such as anxiety disorders, the therapy was very successful.

One of behaviourism's most positive contributions was its adherence to empirical testing and reporting of its studies and findings. This has led to testing now being widely used in different psychological treatments in order to verify proposed clinical outcomes.

In the 1960s, an eminent American psychiatrist, Aaron (Tim) Beck, was becoming increasingly disillusioned with psychoanalytical therapy and what he considered to be its lack of efficacy. Beck became extremely curious about the emotions his clients exhibited that didn't seem to relate to the stories about their childhoods that they were telling him.

Beck became fascinated by what he called 'parallel thought processes' (in effect, the client would be saying one thing, but thinking another) and the fact that the emotions they evoked were related to the patient's conscious mind and to the 'here and now', rather than to the mystique of a long-lost childhood. Beck discovered that many of his clients had similar thoughts quite regularly in their interactions with other people. By working with clients' conscious thought processes – as he called it, 'turning on the intercom' – he was able to obtain very precise definitions of the clients' key problems.

Thus the seeds of cognitive therapy were born – the idea that your conscious thought processes affect how you feel.

At around the same time, another US psychiatrist, Albert Ellis, was also developing a cognitive model, rational emotive therapy (later to become rational emotive behaviour therapy – REBT). Together with Beck, Ellis became one of the most influential pioneers of cognitive therapy – sharing the view that most disturbances arise from thinking errors and faulty processing, and that the remedy is to challenge and re-evaluate thoughts and make behavioural adjustments. Both Beck's CBT and Ellis' REBT were directed at correcting these faulty thought processes. Both concentrated on current problems and present thinking as opposed to past history that was the cornerstone of other psychotherapies, and both incorporated the use of behavioural experimentation.

A new style of therapy

Since its development in the 1960s, cognitive theory has been widely researched – not the least by Beck's own Institute for Cognitive Therapy and Research, which flourishes in Pennsylvania – and treatment protocols have been developed to treat most psychological disorders.

CBT is now the treatment of choice for a wide range of psychological problems. Its boundaries are being consistently enlarged and developed, while its basic principles remain unchanged. It is widely used within the UK's NHS, and recognized as a fast and effective problem solver and life enhancer. If CBT has been around since the 1960s, why has it only in recent years been seen as such an important mainstream therapy, currently in very high demand?

* **The rise in popularity of therapy generally for offering helpful assistance to those in distress.**
* **Past generations may have been brought up with 'keep a stiff upper lip' and 'you simply get on with it' approaches.** In the present day, things have changed greatly and people are much more open about expressing how they feel and discussing their emotions.

* **The value of measurement.** CBT can prove its efficacy by its ability to be empirically measured.
* **The mid-1990s onwards have also seen a huge increase in 'positive psychologies'** – therapy models that are not only interested in how to help people out of specific personal difficulties, but that are also practised to teach people to further enhance lives that already work reasonably.

CBT has fitted the bill here exactly. Compared to insight-based therapies, such as psychodynamic therapy, CBT is a solution-focused, short-term therapy, and because it involves the client in doing a great deal of work for themselves, CBT is an educational model – results are quick, effective and lasting.

However, none of this is to deny other therapies and, naturally, CBT has had its fair share of criticisms as well. Here are some of them and some reasons why we believe they don't hold true.

* **CBT is only helpful to the articulate and intelligent.** CBT is a very flexible model, and is able to completely match the pace of thinking and intellectual level of anyone using it.
* **CBT is simply common sense.** CBT is indeed a logical and understandable therapy – which is one of its great assets. However, its purpose is not just to teach you common-sense solutions, but also to ask a much more important question: 'If the solutions are obvious, what is preventing you from acting on them?'
* **CBT does not focus enough on emotions.** Certainly, there can be a large practical element to treatment, depending on the problem, but this does not mean that a practical solution cannot positively affect a person's emotions.
* **CBT is not interested in important background information about the client's past.** CBT is interested in a client's past, but only in order to discover how they may have developed certain beliefs and assumptions that are unhelpful to them in the present time.

Further applications and developments in cognitive behavioural therapy

The enormous number of applications of CBT extends far beyond those described within the scope of this book. Eating disorders, relationship problems, substance misuse, bipolar disorder, agoraphobia, chronic fatigue syndrome, sexual problems and psychosis, borderline personality disorder, avoidant personality disorder paranoia and schizophrenia – to list a few – are all examples of psychological problems that respond well to CBT. Its applications can be used with a diverse population and in a variety of settings and, at this point, we simply want to alert you to the versatility of CBT – it goes far beyond the foundations of the therapy that we give you here.

CBT protocols are also developing widely, and associated therapies now include (but are not limited to) schema-focused therapy, compassion-based therapy, mindfulness-based cognitive therapy (MBCT), dialectical behaviour therapy, acceptance and commitment therapy, and behavioural activation.

Formulating problems

In cognitive behavioural therapy (CBT), the case formulation (or map or conceptualization, as it can be called) is the driving force of the therapy process, and you can learn to use this yourself.

Defining the problem

Before you can tackle your problems, you need to identify what they are. For some, this may be easy and straightforward. However, sometimes, identifying what is wrong in an exact way is extremely difficult. A common problem can be that of not being able to define exactly why you feel as you do. Some problems might be clear-cut, such as financial difficulties or relationship problems that are easily identifiable. Other problems may be harder to define and can be expressed in more general terms, such as feelings of isolation or worries about the future.

Helping you to understand what is going on

Formulating your problems is a means of helping you to understand them and understand what maintains them from a cognitive behavioural standpoint. It also helps you to understand what may have caused the problems in the first place. At its simplest, a formulation focuses on negative cycles that link thoughts and emotions. Nonetheless, you will constantly change and add to this 'map' of your difficulties.

Think of this map as a piece of plasticine where you are able to constantly change its shape and appearance when new information comes to light that may cause you to want to adjust your ideas and perceptions.

A good map will answer the questions you might be asking, such as:

* Why me?
* Why now?
* Why won't my difficulties go away?
* What do I need to do to feel better?

Formulating your problems will increase your sense of understanding and control over them, which will also help you to avoid them cropping up again in the future.

Idiosyncratic thinking

Everyone has different ways of interpreting their experiences. Different people give their own interpretation to the same experience. This is why discovering the meaning to you of what has happened or might happen is all-important. Unfortunately, we don't always interpret experiences in ways that help us, and the task of CBT is to consider our interpretations and appraise them to see how well they fit with reality and how well they help us.

How to start creating your own map

The vital ingredient of your map is the personal meaning to you of what you think and what you do. Find a recent, *specific* event that had a negative impact on you and work out what was going through your mind, how you felt, how you behaved – and what the outcome of all this was. The outcome might have been a consequence of your actions and reactions, but it might also be simply the meaning you have placed on the series of events.

Figure 1.1 will, almost certainly, bear no relation at all to your own concerns or circumstances, but it will show you how to fill out your own route map.

Some questions to help you develop your own map

If you are feeling depressed or anxious, ask yourself:
* What am I depressed or anxious about?
* What situations or life events have led me to feel this way?
* What are the thoughts that contribute to these feelings that overwhelm me?

Also think about answers to the following:
* What are my current problems?
* How did these develop?
* When did they develop?
* How are my problems being maintained?
* What thoughts, ideas and beliefs do I have that support the problems?
* What reactions do I have in association with these thoughts – emotionally (how I feel), behaviourally (how I behave) and physiologically (bodily tension, fatigue)?

Look at the outline in Figure 1.1, and then use the answers to the above questions to fill in your own map.

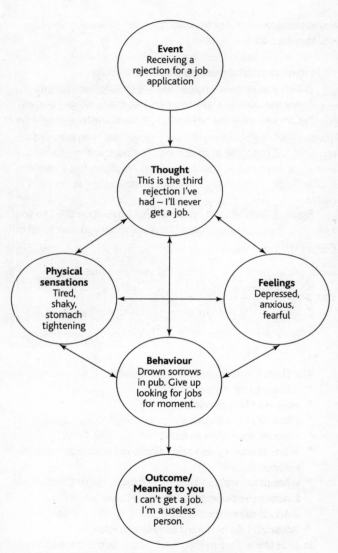

Figure 1.1 *An example formulation/conceptualization.*

Interpretation

Ask yourself the following questions:

* Can you see the link between thoughts, feelings, behaviour and physical sensations?
* Can you see what is maintaining the problem for you?
* Are you able to identify a personal meaning for yourself?
* Can you work out where this personal meaning might have come from?

Making connections: joining the dots

You are now becoming familiar with the idea that CBT practice involves observing your responses to disturbing situations and then drawing your attention to the connection between cognitions, moods and behaviours. Because thoughts, feelings and actions are all connected, making changes for the better in any one area will have a positive effect on the other areas.

You will find the easiest way to develop conceptualizations of your problems is to ask yourself questions such as these:

* **What is the life situation that is disturbing me?**
  * Has something happened recently?
  * Looking back over the last few years, what has distressed me most?
  * Going back to my youth or childhood, can I identify any ongoing difficulties?
* **How do I feel about this?**
  * Identify your emotions specifically, for example, angry, sad, anxious, depressed.
* **What thoughts do I have about this?**
  * About myself?
  * About others?
  * About the situation?
  * About the future?
* **What do I do in regard to this situation?**
  * Simply accept it?
  * Use avoidance where I can?

- Act in a way that doesn't seem to make a positive difference?
- Do the best I can, but it still doesn't help?

Use your basic route map (formulation/conceptualization) to work through a variety of specific situations. You will begin to see a pattern in your responses and to identify certain beliefs (more on those later) that may contribute to the maintenance of your problems.

Turning problems into goals

Identifying the problem is a start. Once the problem or problems are defined, you are then in a position to look at what you can do to improve the situation by creating and developing your goals.

Cognitive behavioural therapy (CBT) is a structured therapy. Where you are working with a professional therapist, the early sessions will be used, in part, for working with you to define specifically and clearly:

* what your problems are
* what is maintaining your problems
* how you would like things to be and what you will need to change to achieve this.

Setting goals isn't always as easy as it appears

Often, knowing what we don't want is easier than knowing what we do want. Moreover, setting goals that are too grandiose or too hard to achieve can be dispiriting rather than rewarding. So, learning the skills of successful goal-setting is extremely important, right at the start. This does not mean that your goals will be 'set in stone'. Good goals have built-in flexibility to be adjusted as you, your life and your personal desires change.

Working out your goals

Your goals might be something like this:
* I wish I was in a committed relationship.
* I wish my finances were in better order.

* I wish I could get a promotion at work.
* I wish I got on better with my family.

And if they were, your therapist would ask you to rewrite them, taking out the word 'wish' and replacing it with 'would like'.

Wishing and hoping get you nowhere. Stating what you would actually like is much more positive, and a better starting point for change.

It is also quite okay, and sometimes easier, to put down what you don't want, rather than what you do. For example:

* I don't want to keep feeling anxious.
* I don't want to be in the same job a year from now.
* I don't want to be on my own for ever.
* I hate feeling so low all the time.
* I wish I wasn't ill any more.

These types of goals are often referred to as 'Dead Man's Goals', that is, this could be achieved by a dead man – no more anxious feelings, no more job worries, etc. You need to turn them into more positive aspirations by simply turning them around. For example, turn 'I don't want to keep feeling anxious' into 'I would like to feel more confident and worry less about things'.

Setting priorities

The goals now need to be prioritized so that what is more important is at the top of the list, and the things that are less important are of a lower ranking. One of the mistakes people can make when trying to change things is that they become grasshoppers, hopping from one thing to another the whole time and never giving total focus to one specific thing.

The goals can be divided into two sub-sections:
* those which can only be achieved by doing something
* those which might be achieved by thinking differently.

The SMART way to set goals

Some of you may have used the SMART goal-setting tool before – it is extremely helpful in your quest to focus, to make things specific, so that you can be sure that a goal is exactly the goal that you want and can weigh up whether it is realistic.

SMART goals have all of these qualities:

* **Specific.** This means rejecting generalizations, such as 'I would like to be happier', 'I would like to feel better about myself', and focusing on exactly what you want.

* **Measurable.** How will you know if you have achieved your goal? What will be different?

* **Achievable.** People waste a great deal of time and energy wishing and dreaming about things that, for the huge majority of us, are just never going to happen. Always ask yourself, 'If all else goes as it should, is this within my grasp?' If the answer is 'Yes', you have something to work with.

* **Realistic.** Where your goals are realistic, not only do you achieve them, but you get a 'feel-good' factor from the achievement, which boosts your confidence.

Another way in which your goals need to be realistic is that they have to be within your control.

* **Time frame.** Always set a time frame – if you don't, then your motivation will slip away and you won't feel the joys of succeeding as you had planned. Set good, realistic time frames for your goals.

Finally the goals need to be rated from 'Hardest to achieve' to 'Easiest to achieve', and those in between. The issue of which goals to tackle first will be resolved by the Easy/Hard ratings. It is helpful to tackle first easier goals and those where change is likely to occur quite rapidly, in order to boost hope and confidence.

2

*thoughts
and
moods*

Just as what you think decides how you feel, the reverse is also true: how you feel dictates what you think. Physical responses are linked to moods.

Thoughts, emotions and actions are all interlinked and when you change in one area of your formulation, it changes other areas too. Therefore, when your mood changes, you think about things differently, and vice versa.

Thoughts can be positive, neutral, evaluative and action-orientated. It is the underlying thoughts and beliefs that are the true cause of associated strong emotion. Different levels of thoughts can be captured for later analysis.

Negative thoughts can be a major cause of anxiety and depression. They cannot be blocked out, but can be challenged and replaced by more balanced alternative beliefs.

Becoming familiar with moods and being able to match an appropriate emotion with the particular situation is the key to developing 'emotional intelligence'.

In Chapter 1, you learned how to describe what is going on in a way that helps you to see that negative thoughts, feelings and behaviour simply perpetuate a problem rather than improve or get rid of it. The good thing about a formulation is that you can go into any part of it and make changes, and the changes you make to that particular area — say your behaviour — will have a positive effect on each other area. However, it is most usual to start by looking at negative thoughts and making changes there, at least to begin with. Consequently, you now need to learn how to identify, specifically, what you are actually thinking that causes you emotional distress.

Capturing thoughts

Many people have great problems in identifying their thinking. Some even say, 'Nothing is going through my mind' or 'I can't come up with anything'. Sometimes, it really is very difficult to access your worrying thoughts, and you may possibly feel that you simply don't know what was in your mind, it was simply an emotion, sitting there on its own.

Firstly, how many types of thoughts do you think you have? Many people believe we simply have negative thoughts and positive thoughts. While, when things go wrong, we find it easy to identify negative thoughts, what other types of thoughts can you identify? Here are some ideas:

* **Positive thoughts:** 'Everything is going really well.'
* **Neutral thoughts:** 'I wonder what to have for lunch today?'
* **Evaluative thoughts:** 'Is this the best way to do that?'
* **Action-oriented thoughts:** 'I'm going to solve this problem...'
* **Rational thoughts:** 'While I initially believed this to be true, I can now see that there are alternatives.'

You are now acquainted with the idea that what we think decides how we feel. However, this is just as true in reverse — how we feel decides what we think. You may therefore find it easier to identify your mood first, and then work out what the thoughts might be that have caused it.

Exercise

This exercise will help you to identify your thoughts through recognizing your moods. You are to create a simple 'Thought Record' like the one on page 22. Thought Records are a basic tool of cognitive behavioural therapy and help to clarify thinking and feelings.

To help you identify your mood, look for physical sensations. Check first with any bodily changes – are you feeling tired and lethargic (when it is likely that your mood will be low, or depressed)? Is your stomach churning and your heart racing (when it is likely that your mood will be anxious or panicky)?

Write your identified mood in the 'Feelings' column of the Thought Record – you may wish to write down more than one. Then write down what is happening or has just happened to make you feel this way in the second column. Finally, write down what is going through your mind or was going through your mind just before this happened in the third column.

We have asked you to write down your mood before anything else as it will be the strongest part of the situation. Once you have expressed how you feel, you can then write down why – what was happening, what you thought. You can ask yourself some simple questions to assist you. For example:

* 'What was I afraid might be going to happen?'
* 'What was happening or was in my mind just before I began feeling this way?'
* 'Am I recalling any past incidences where things turned out poorly?'

What was the trigger? The 'Situation' column in a Thought Record is very important. It enables you to begin to see patterns in 'trigger points' that more readily engender negative thoughts and emotions. This is excellent information for you as it allows you to adjust the situation or even, if it is sensible and possible, eliminate it. If you cannot do either of these things, you will at least be aware ahead of time of possible mood changes and you can therefore create an action plan to help you overcome your negative thoughts and feelings.

Thought Record

Feelings	Situation	Thought(s)
For example, *angry, sad, despairing, anxious.*	This may be an actual event, or just an image in your mind.	What was going through your mind just before you began to feel this way?
Circle the strongest of your feelings.		If you have put down more than one thought, circle the strongest.
Nervous Irritated (Fearful)	*Awaiting annual appraisal at work from a boss I don't especially get on with.*	*I'm sure my appraisal won't be good. My boss is always a difficult person who will cut me no slack.* *Supposing it's so bad that I am given a warning?*

Identifying your strongest thoughts and feelings

In the Thought Record, you should circle the strongest emotion and thought where perhaps you have written down several. This is to ensure that:

* you focus on the thoughts and feelings that bother you the most
* your thoughts and feelings 'match'.

'Matching' thoughts and moods is exceedingly important. Many people waste weeks and months filling in Thought Records that are of no help to them because they do not correctly identify and work on the critical thought that is engendering the emotion.

Identifying the causal thought

An excellent way to ensure that you don't waste time on the wrong thought is to rate your thoughts and emotions, either from 1 to 10, or by using a percentage figure. For example, if your mood rating is 'Panic (90%)', a negative thought on the lines of, 'My friend has forgotten our lunch appointment' is not going to be the causal thought – that is, the thought that triggers the emotion. Ask yourself, 'Why does that matter?' and you are more likely to get to the correct causal thought, which in this case could be, 'Perhaps she has been involved in a serious accident'.

The downward arrow technique:

This is an excellent skill for capturing causal thoughts. Here is an example.

You are feeling stressed, anxious and your head is aching. Your thought is: 'I can't seem to get on with the work I need to do for this presentation.'

Isn't that it? Many people would stop right there: you are feeling exceedingly stressed (say 80%) and the reason is that you cannot get on with the work you need to do. That makes sense. But, from the exercise you completed above, you now know that isn't the case. Not being able to get on with your work might be bothersome, but that might irritate you only a little, and not account for such a high stress level. To work out why it is the cause of such highly rated emotion, you ask yourself a further question, as shown in Figure 2.1.

Now you have a causal thought. You have arrived at a thought that makes complete sense in the context of feeling such a high degree of emotion. This is crucial – it means you have identified exactly what you need to work on.

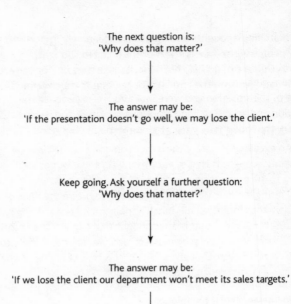

The next question is:
'Why does that matter?'

↓

The answer may be:
'If the presentation doesn't go well, we may lose the client.'

↓

Keep going. Ask yourself a further question:
'Why does that matter?'

↓

The answer may be:
'If we lose the client our department won't meet its sales targets.'

↓

Don't stop. Ask a third question:
'Why does that matter?'

↓

The answer may be:
'I'll be held responsible and I may even lose my job.'

Figure 2.1 *Downward arrow technique.*

Using imagery

Sometimes it is much easier to capture a thought when you imagine yourself in the situation that caused strong emotion. Particularly in situations of high anxiety, the strength of the mood can be overpowering. Picture yourself in the situation. Recreate in your mind what was going on around you and how you were feeling. Close your eyes if that helps. Relive the situation as closely as you can. Notice various aspects of where you are. If you are indoors, notice pictures on the walls, for example, or the type of furniture in the room. This will help you to recreate an accurate image of the situation you were in. As you re-experience the situation and accompanying emotions, you may find it easier to identify the thoughts that were going through your mind.

Testing the validity of your thinking

We all have a natural propensity to think in a certain way. Some find it easy to have an optimistic, positive outlook. Others are more cautious and weigh up pros and cons carefully. Yet others tend to think automatically in a more negative, pessimistic way. We are not sure why this is. It may be due to our biological or genetic inheritance, but also – most often – to our environment: our upbringing, early adulthood and specific, meaningful events. All these come together to develop our thinking style.

Once you understand that not all your thinking is helpful to you and that many of your thoughts actually hinder you, it makes sense to try to find more constructive ways of viewing yourself, others and the world around you.

Cognitive behavioural therapy (CBT) is based on the understanding that people construct their own realities and have idiosyncratic ways of interpreting their experiences. Different people give their own interpretation to an experience. You can see this in the way that children from the same family will recall aspects of their childhood differently – the same events took place but each interprets what happened in their own unique way. People can respond differently to the same situation, and this is usually because of their own, personal, often deeply-held beliefs about themselves, other people and the world.

Unfortunately, people don't always interpret experiences in ways that help them. Negative thinking can create problems for everyone from time to time, and CBT helps you to identify unhelpful thought patterns and beliefs, and to find alternative ways of thinking and perceiving that work for you. So how do you make a start?

Introducing negative automatic thoughts (NATs)

Pessimistic, negative thoughts, such as 'I can't cope' or 'I feel terrible', only make you feel more anxious and unhappy and can themselves be a major cause of anxiety or depression. Some of your thoughts may be based on reality, but some will probably be 'guesswork', and you may be jumping to conclusions that paint things blacker than they are. We call these 'negative automatic thoughts' (NATs) because they are unrealistically pessimistic and because they seem to come from nowhere and 'automatically' enter your mind.

NATs are just like a chatterbox going on in your head. You haven't invited these thoughts in, and you often wish they would leave, but instead, they stay there, talking at you like a radio you cannot switch off. One error that you can make with NATs is to try to block them out. Yet the more you wish they weren't there, the more they cling to you and dominate your thinking. Why is this?

Try a small experiment

Sit for one minute and during that time you **must not once** think about the word 'giraffe'. Not once.

What happened? We guess that your mind was flooded with giraffes – and that the more you tried to block the thoughts, the more giraffes there were.

Once you ascribe a meaning to your thought and try to block it out, it doubles and quadruples in your mind. However, when it doesn't matter whether you have a particular thought or not, when it can come or go as it pleases, you don't notice it, and it doesn't bother you.

This is a very important lesson as CBT is not about controlling your thinking and blocking out negative thoughts. You would have very little success with this. CBT is about taking a long, hard look at the validity of your thoughts and then re-evaluating them, offering yourself more rational, balanced alternatives.

Becoming aware of negative thoughts

Becoming aware of these thoughts can help you to understand why your moods are negative. This is the first step towards learning to think in a more helpful, positive way. To help you to do this, you first need to know a little more about what negative thoughts 'look like'. The following is a list of characteristics that these thoughts have in common.

* They spring to mind without any effort from you.
* They are easy to believe.
* They are often not true.
* They can be difficult to stop.
* They are unhelpful.
* They keep you anxious or depressed and make it difficult to change.

Thought Records and negative automatic thoughts

You can examine your NATs by using a Thought Record. The more you practise filling in Thought Records, the easier it becomes to spot these NATs and to understand the effect they have on how you feel.

Don't worry if you find this difficult at first. It may be quite a new idea to try to remember what you were thinking when you were worried or feeling low, and it may take some practice before you get the hang of it. Next time you find yourself becoming tense, worried or depressed, as soon as you can, sit down and fill in your Thought Record. Describe the physical sensations you experienced and the thoughts that went through your head at the time.

On the right is an example of a good basic Thought Record.

Five-column Thought Record example

What happened?	How you felt when this happened	What you thought	Alternative thoughts	How do you feel now?
What were you doing or thinking about?	What did you feel? How bad was it? (%)	What exactly were your thoughts? How far did you believe them? (%)	What more positive alternative thoughts can you think of? Try to find as many as you can. How far do you believe each one? (%)	How far do you now still believe your negative thoughts? (%) Do you feel any better emotionally now, i.e. less downhearted? (%)
Staying away with a friend for a few days.	*Anxiety (100%) Panic (80%) Fear (100%)*	*I shall not be able to cope. (100%) If I feel sick, I won't know what to do. (90%) The journey there will be difficult. (60%)*	*This is a nice opportunity to relax. (60%) I have made perfectly adequate arrangements in case I feel unwell. (60%) It will be a treat to get away to a lovely part of the country. (70%)*	*The journey was fine. We all got on very well. I did not feel sick or anxious. I managed well in every way. I feel fine. (100%)*

Action plan: Remain more relaxed in these situations, and do not always jump to negative conclusions too quickly.

Don't worry too much if you are having trouble consigning your negative thoughts to the rubbish bin. This Thought Record is just the start of learning new ways of challenging your self-defeating thinking. Your new beliefs will strengthen in time. This is also just one of many skills you will be learning that will help you to feel much better.

Talking back to your negative thoughts

You will see that the Thought Record on page 28 has more columns than the one on page 22. Not only are you recording your negative thoughts and feelings, but you can now keep track of them and examine how unrealistic or unhelpful they are and whether they are useful to you. If they are unrealistic or unhelpful, you can challenge them with what we call a 'balanced response'. This is a reply that you can make to these thoughts, based on firm evidence.

'But it really is that way'

NATs are not necessarily always invalid. Many people think that the point of CBT is to identify your negative thoughts as faulty or skewed, and then to search for more positive replacements that will, in turn, make you feel better. While this can sometimes be the case, it is not always so. CBT's role is essentially to help you to critically evaluate your NATs in the light of possible alternatives, and to come to a balanced and rational conclusion about the strength of their validity.

The difficulty of finding alternative thoughts

Sometimes it can be very hard to find balanced alternatives to the negative thoughts you have, because you actually are in a jam or a tight spot. You did give in poor work when you got lambasted by the boss, or you did behave selfishly when you might have been kind.

An action plan to help you

You will notice at the bottom of your Thought Record that there is a small section entitled 'Action plan'. When, having looked at all the options, you are faced with accepting that your negative thoughts are very close to the mark, your solution is to develop an action plan. You need to ask yourself what you might be able to do to mitigate what has happened, and identify a variety of different options for putting things right.

Coping statements as a positive tool

Occasionally, simply acknowledging the truth of the predicament you find yourself in and using coping statements, rather than alternative thoughts, can be the most helpful thing. Here are some examples of coping statements that, while acknowledging that your negative thinking may have some validity, nonetheless still enable you to deal with your worries in a more positive and constructive way.

* 'I'm going to face this problem situation so that I can practise coping better.'
* 'It may not work completely, but the important thing is to practise and build up my confidence.'
* 'I know that worry makes me feel worse. I know that I can manage my feelings.'
* 'I've been in this position before and have come out of it in one piece.'
* 'I know things will improve the more I get used to coping with my difficulties.'
* 'I'll feel proud of myself when I feel myself getting calmer and more confident.'
* 'It feels good learning how to control worrying feelings.'
* 'I'm deliberately going to change how I feel.'

Practice makes perfect

The key to being able to think in a more balanced way is to keep practising. Every time you become aware of negative thoughts going through your mind, stop yourself and think of a more balanced, realistic response. When preparing to go into a situation that makes you anxious or worried, think about how you will answer any negative thoughts before, during and afterwards.

My alternative thoughts don't help me feel better

Writing out more balanced, optimistic alternatives to your NATs may cause you to think more broadly than you have done before – but you may also find that, on balance, you don't really believe what you are writing, and your NAT stays firmly entrenched in your mind. If you find this to be the case:

* Consider whether your alternative thoughts are specific and realistic, or whether they are 'Pollyanna thinking'. Make your alternative thoughts something you have genuine belief in.
* You may need to test out your alternative thoughts in order to increase your belief in them. You can do this by thinking about the evidence you may have to support them, or by using behavioural experiments that will give you more concrete evidence about them.

More on moods

Identifying moods

Moods are not always as easy to identify as you might think. Many clients we have worked with have discovered only through using cognitive behavioural therapy (CBT) detective work that they have actually suffered from low mood or depression for years. They failed to recognize it since they were unaware of what it might be like to feel differently. Sometimes, simply feeling tired all the time can be indicative of depression; or feeling constantly tense and wound up can be caused by a generally anxious state of mind.

Before you can make changes, you need to be able to do two things:

1 Be aware of your emotions.
2 Identify the appropriate emotions for the particular situation you are in.

Your first indicator

The first thing to consider when identifying your mood is how your body feels. What is going on when your heart starts beating a little fast, or your breathing is shallow? Notice changes in your body that will give you an indication that you are beginning to feel an emotion of some sort.

Although we are focusing on the detrimental effects of negative emotions in this book, considering the physical effect of positive emotions will also be helpful. Think about a time when something good happened. Perhaps you received a letter giving good news about a job application, or an unexpected invitation to a pleasurable event. Recall how you felt on such an occasion, and the effect it might have had on your body. Think about flushed cheeks, an automatic smile, tenseness deserting you, and your heart beating faster with joy rather than dread.

Becoming more emotionally aware

Becoming more emotionally aware is a huge first step in learning to manage your emotions. It is a great skill, not simply when things are going badly and you need to work on that, but in life generally. We call this being 'emotionally intelligent'. In simple terms, this means being able to:

* identify correctly what you are feeling
* evaluate the appropriateness of the emotion to the situation
* manage how you feel so that inappropriate emotions don't 'run away' with you.

Knowing how you feel

Sometimes it is not easy to ascribe emotions to your thoughts. Emotions can be a little more comprehensive than you might imagine. For example, you could describe yourself as 'happy'. Yet under the 'feeling happy' umbrella is a variety of what you might call 'meta-emotions' — jolly, playful, jubilant, thrilled, exhilarated.

Be as honest as you can

A common difficulty that everyone has is being honest with themselves. Even when you are working to uncover emotions that you know will be helpful, it can still be difficult to own up to yourself that you feel guilty, selfish, angry, ashamed or jealous. You may be tempted – even within the privacy of your own mind – to excuse how you feel by giving a different label to the moods that are driving you. If you find yourself feeling this way, you can use the thought-challenging skills that you have now learned to work through this. For example:

My NAT: 'I don't want to admit to myself that I am jealous or selfish. It simply makes me feel bad about myself, so I would rather not go there.'

My rational responses:

* 'There is nothing wrong in feeling such emotions. We are all fallible human beings, and we all, from time to time, succumb to selfishness, jealousy and other emotions that we are not too proud of.'
* 'Simply recognizing these emotions and admitting to them is half the battle. Many people wouldn't.'
* 'Once I have properly owned these emotions I can begin to make changes. If I don't do this, they will stick around and everything will stay the same.'

Faulty thinking styles

Many of the negative thoughts and feelings that you have about yourself are caused by what we call 'cognitive bias' – patterns of distorted thinking. Learning to recognize these patterns is a useful skill as you will then be able to recognize a great many of your individual NATs as one of these thinking styles. Then, challenging them becomes much easier.

Recognizing distorted thinking is not always easy. People assume that all their thinking is rational and correct even when it is negative. In a good frame of mind it may be (though not always). Yet when you are in a poor frame of mind, your thinking can become distorted without you realizing this is happening.

Compounding thinking errors

The problem is that once you start making thinking errors, you tend to 'stick with them'. They become assumptions and beliefs (more on these soon) that are retained, unless an effort is made to identify and change them.

Psychologists have identified a number of common thinking errors that most people make some of the time (and some people make all of the time). If you know what these are, and recognize them, it will make your thought-challenging rebuttals much easier to formulate. Read through the thinking errors below and place a tick against any you feel apply to you.

Generalizing the specific

You generalize the specific when you come to a general conclusion, based on a single incident or piece of evidence. You use words such as 'always' and 'never', 'nobody' and 'everyone' to make an all-embracing rule out of a specific situation. If you make a mistake, you tell yourself that you are hopeless. If you get rejected, you tell yourself that you are unlovable.

Mind reading

This is one of the most common thinking errors people make when self-esteem is low. Without other people saying so, you 'know' what they are thinking, why they act the way they do and how people are feeling towards you. This is fatal to self-esteem because you believe that others agree with your negative opinions of yourself. Yet you are jumping to conclusions without any real evidence – and, you only seem to have the gift of mind-reading *negative* views not for positive thoughts!

Magnification and filtering

You take the negative details from a situation and then magnify them, while at the same time filtering out all the positive aspects. You focus on the one thing that went badly in an otherwise successful presentation. You dismiss all your achievements and focus bleakly on the one thing that you are not so good at.

Polarized thinking

Sometimes called 'all or nothing thinking', you think of people, situations or events in extremes such as good or bad – 'I must be perfect or I am a failure', 'If I'm not beautiful, I'm ugly'. There is no middle ground. The problem is that you usually find yourself at the negative end of your polarized extremes. So if you cannot be all good, you must be all bad.

Catastrophizing

You expect disaster. You believe that things will almost certainly go wrong if they possibly can – and that if they do you will not be able to cope. Not only do you over-estimate the likelihood of calamity, you multiply it by your perceived idea of the catastrophic consequences. Whenever you notice or hear about a problem, you start on 'What if's and then decide that if this terrible thing did happen to you, you would not be able to cope.

Personalization

This involves thinking that everything people do or say is some kind of reaction to you.

Blaming

This is the opposite of personalization. You hold other people, organizations – or even the universe – responsible for your problems. You feel unable to change your views or your circumstances, as you see yourself as a victim of other people's thoughtlessness and meanness.

Self-blame

In this case, instead of feeling a victim, you feel responsible for the pain and happiness of everyone around you.

Rigid thinking

You feel resentful because you think you know what's right, but other people won't agree with you. You continually attempt to prove that your opinions and actions are correct. You expect other people to change their views and actions if you pressure or cajole them enough. You try to change people in this way when you believe your hopes for happiness depend entirely on their behaving differently.

A positive way forward

While it can be hard to discover that much of your thinking is biased by negative distortions, acknowledging this is the first step to change. The next step is to use this knowledge to help you tackle your thoughts. How? By working to familiarize yourself with these cognitive distortions. Once you understand them and can recall them easily, you can begin to spot them when they crop up. They are easier for you to identify than some of your NATs because of the patterns they follow, and you can take an, 'Oh, I recognize what I'm doing!' attitude to them and then rethink what has actually happened.

Most people, when presented with these styles of distorted thinking and asked to acknowledge any that apply to them, find themselves actually smiling as they recognize these common thinking errors. They are normal! We all do it. Now you can become more aware of them and knock them on the head quite easily.

3

adjusting your thinking

Thought Records are flexible, useful tools which can be adapted to accommodate a variety of thought challenging and behavioural testing. Negative thoughts can be challenged by looking for evidence to support or refute them.

Behaviour mirrors thinking, and thoughts, emotions and actions impact on each other. Behavioural experiments are a way of testing alternative thoughts and actions to find out what works for a person.

By reaching down into our thought processes we can uncover our core beliefs. These are thought patterns that lie beneath your assumptions, personal rules and negative automatic thoughts as absolute and rigid truths. They may have developed in childhood and been fortified by experiences from other times in your life.

We sometimes impose demands on ourselves that are difficult to meet. They may seem useful as a motivational tool but they have the opposite effect, giving a sense of failure. We need to accept the idea of human fallibility.

Checking for evidence

How can you strengthen your belief in your alternative views?

There is one extremely helpful tool — regarded by cognitive behavioural therapy (CBT) practitioners as one of the most important and valuable 'thought shifters' around. It asks a simple question: 'If this is really so, where's the evidence?'

When your mood is low or your thoughts are filled with anxiety, you focus on the negative and ignore the positive evidence. So we want you to introduce this element into your Thought Record.

To help you to practise this skill, look back to your most recent negative thought.

* Ask yourself what evidence you had to support it.
* If you were a barrister in a court of law, could you provide evidence against it?
* What would you say?

Giving evidence in your Thought Record

Think of your Thought Record as a 'flexible friend' — it can be adapted to accommodate a wide variety of thought challenging and behavioural testing (see later). What you have now (see opposite) is a full, basic, seven-column Thought Record.

Seven-column Thought Record

The first extra column asks you to find evidence to support your NATs, and the second to support your alternative, balanced responses.

Why look for evidence to support negative thinking first? It might seem to make more sense to simply find evidence to support an alternative, more positive thought than to search for

What happened?	What you thought when this happened (How strongly do you believe this? 1–10)	How you felt (How strongly did you feel this? 1–10)	Evidence to support your negative thoughts	Alternative thoughts (Generate at least two or three alternatives. Rate your belief in them 1–10)	Evidence to support your alternative thoughts	How do you feel now? (Rate any possible change now you have looked at things a little more positively. 1–10)

evidence to support your negative thinking. However, we ask you to do this first because, at this stage, you will have a strong belief that your negative thoughts are true. To start by looking for evidence that these strong thoughts are not true may be difficult and you may lack conviction. It is too far away from how you may presently see things. If you truly believe that you are a bad parent, for example, you will find it easier to search out evidence to support that view, and then to question the validity of that evidence, than to simply search for opposites. For instance, such evidence might include, 'I shout at my kids a lot', 'I don't spend enough time with them', and so on. When you start to find more optimistic alternatives, you now have something to work with. You might be able to say to yourself, 'I only shout at my kids when I'm tired, and lots of parents do that' or 'When I am not actually with them, I am working for their benefit'. You should then be able to find evidence that will support these alternatives and make sense.

You may find it harder than you think to come up with solid reasoning. Where you consider that you have evidence to support your NATs (which you may well do) then you need to support them with:

* data
* facts
* experiences.

You cannot support them simply with opinions — either yours or anyone else's. Good questions to ask yourself before you commit your evidence to paper are:

* 'What would a judge think of my evidence?'
* 'Would "Oh, I just can't help thinking that way" stand up in a court of law?'
* 'Would the judge accept it or throw it out?'

Finding evidence for your alternative thinking will be easier when you have worked through the other Thought Record columns. For example, imagine you have looked in the mirror just before going out and thought, 'I look dreadful.'

An alternative thought might be, 'I really don't look too bad.' But the strength of your belief in this would probably be weak. Your belief will become much stronger if you write down any evidence that might genuinely support your more balanced thought.

As you get used to finding evidence for your thinking, it will loosen your NATs' hold on your mind through tangible, logical argument, rather than simply repeating optimistic alternatives that you don't *truly* feel hold water. This is a very powerful skill.

Search hard

Finding evidence can – and should – involve effort on your part. It is the most important tool you will have among your CBT skills for successfully challenging and replacing invalid thoughts. Don't simply give it lip service. Think of the painstaking way that detectives search for clues and evidence, to help them come to the correct conclusion about a crime.

Focusing bias

When people think in a negative way about something, they tend to focus on and believe in data that supports this view. Evidence to support an alternative view can often be outside of their awareness and they need to search hard for it.

The importance of behaviour in the cognitive model

If you look again at any conceptualizations you drew up that reflected situations and outcomes personal to you, you will notice that how you behaved had a great effect on maintaining how you felt and what you thought. We call this 'self-defeating behaviour'. For example, if someone with low self-esteem is turned down for a job they want very badly, they may say to themselves, 'I'm useless.

I'll never get a good job. There will always be other candidates far better than me.' In this negative thinking state, what is this person's most likely *behavioural* response? The likelihood is that their behaviour will mirror their *thinking*.

* They may stop applying for jobs altogether.
* They may set their sights lower and apply for jobs below their capabilities.
* They may continue to go for interviews but expect to do badly at them, which will be reflected in the impression they make or fail to make.

This means that this person is likely to remain unemployed – confirming that their negative thoughts and beliefs were correct. This will make the person feel emotionally low, and their self-esteem will sink even lower.

Deciding what to do

Changing your behaviour seems an obvious way forward and upwards, but how can you decide what to do, or be sure that it will give you the results you want? The answer is that you can't – for certain. However, you can develop action plans in the form of behavioural 'experiments' – trying out ideas that you think might be helpful, and checking the result against what you were hoping for. Behavioural experiments can be used for a variety of helpful purposes:

* to test the validity of your thoughts
* to discover, with an open mind, what might happen if you do A instead of B
* to observe outcomes and results of behaviour changes
* to learn to manage your emotions by graded exposure to feared situations.

Your options

In its simplest form, CBT offers three possibilities when you feel disturbed by your views of life events.

1 You can adjust your thinking about what you perceive to be happening or to have happened, moving it from a negative outlook to a more balanced, rational point of view.

2 You can change your behaviour – taking a different approach to a problem to see if you get a better result.

3 You can do nothing, and accept things as they are. Never dismiss this option entirely. Sometimes simply coming to terms with things is a positive way forward in itself.

Guided discovery

Guided discovery is the process by which you test your thinking and your behaviours. You literally try something out and see what happens. You then process what you have learned and, if you consider it helpful, you may wish to continue to think and act in this new way. If you discover that it was not helpful and failed to make you feel better, you discard it.

Negative, self-defeating behaviours can easily be a self-fulfilling prophecy, which is why people may continue to believe in them.

Using a behavioural experiment Thought Record

Overleaf is a slightly 'new style' Thought Record specifically for recording behavioural experiments and their outcomes. In the example given, Lesley, who lacks confidence and normally tries to avoid social situations, decides to try something new – to be just a little more social and to attempt to start a few conversations. It is a nerve-wracking idea for her, and she has no real idea what the result will be. In fact, her prediction of the outcome is very negative. However, she gives it a try and afterwards evaluates what actually happened against her prediction of what would happen. She discovers that things turn out a lot better than she thought, and she is able to learn from this and build on it.

Thought Record for behavioural experiments

Date and situation	Prediction What do you think will happen? How much do you believe it will? (%) How anxious do you feel? (%)	Experiment What can you do to test out your prediction? (ensure you drop all safety behaviours)	Outcome What actually happened? Was the prediction correct? How anxious do you feel now? (%)	What I have learned Is there a more balanced view? How much do you believe your first prediction will happen in the future? How can I build on this?
Walking into a party on my own.	I will feel very embarrassed and no one will speak to me. I'll just want to go home as soon as possible. 80%	I will get myself a drink and then look around for someone I can talk to. I will ask one or two basic questions and then focus on listening to the responses.	I did as I'd planned and, although I felt a little self-conscious, I realized that others felt the same and were very pleased to speak to me. I enjoyed the party and stayed later than I had intended.	Firstly, not to avoid difficult situations. Secondly, that, if I plan a little and stop listening to my negative chatterbox, I can cope with these situations better than I had thought, and actually have quite a nice time. 20%

Designing your own experiments

Think about your own problems – perhaps, like Lesley in the case study above, you suffer from social anxiety. Perhaps you have more generalized anxiety – you simply get nervous easily and there are many things that you fail to try because you make negative predictions as to the outcome. Thus, you never discover either that things don't turn out as badly as you thought, or that you have more resources to cope with them than you realized. The problem here is that you maintain the problem (usually a faulty belief) and that you *compound* it. As with anything, the less you do it, the less confident you become that you could possibly attempt it. Sooner or later, your nervousness about driving on motorways becomes nervousness about driving anywhere. Your worries that you'll play badly when invited to play tennis causes you to give away your rackets and never play again.

What might you like to change?

Think about any perceived weakness you consider you have. Now think how you would like to be. Finally, think about what you could try to see if you can make a positive change.

Your action plan

In Chapter 1 you learned to set goals. Behavioural experiments require you to use some of these goal-setting skills.

Plan your steps

Your experiment should push you a little way outside of your comfort zone, but not too far. Your goal is to succeed, not to set yourself up to fail. For example, if you are nervous of going in lifts (perhaps fearing claustrophobia and panic attacks), your first experiment might be to stand in a lobby where lifts are operating. You might be willing to stand very close to the lift door, or even step inside for a moment. Record how that feels. You are putting yourself in a situation where no harm can come to you, but you may be experiencing some anxiety and you are testing the consequences. You may discover that you did not feel as bad as you thought you would. If this is the case, you may be willing to try another, slightly harder experiment next time – perhaps to go up one floor in a lift and become aware of how you feel. This is called 'graded exposure'.

Plan ahead

Begin to become aware of all the negative predictions you make. Perhaps you don't confront your work colleague about sloppiness because you predict that they will fly off the handle and turn your argument around. In situations like this, advance planning can help you. Decide ahead of time how you might tackle the problem in the best way – and then be willing to test it out.

Visualize it

If the idea of a particular behavioural change seems especially frightening – standing up to your boss or someone who is taking advantage of you; saying 'No' for the first time when you've always said 'Yes' – then use visualization to practise in advance. Sit quietly, close your eyes, and imagine the situation and the behaviour change you would like to make. Picture yourself acting in a different way. See a very clear picture in your mind – notice the surroundings, the details, the colours. This will help to make the visualization more real and accurate. Focus on your feelings after you have visualized yourself dealing with your problem in a new way. Does this make you feel a little more confident? Practise your visualization as many times as you need to in order to feel more comfortable with testing it in reality.

Be proactive

Conducting behavioural experiments requires you to become proactive. It means actually doing something a little different to see if you can get a better result. You have to challenge negative assumptions and predictions, rather than presuming them to be correct (sometimes, of course, they might be; be prepared for this – but never accept them without validation). It means identifying self-defeating behaviour and seeing whether there isn't a better way – a way to make you feel better, to lift your mood, to give you more confidence.

Deeper layers of thinking

The 'top layer': automatic thoughts

One of the features of negative automatic thoughts (NATs) is that they are *event-specific*. That is to say, there is usually a trigger event, which might be something negative you can clearly identify, such as losing a job or a partner, having a quarrel with a friend or having a car accident, etc. The trigger event can be as straightforward as suddenly having an image or idea when you are sitting at home alone in the evening time or doing a spot of gardening. It is the event (in whatever shape or form) that, for one reason or another, engenders negative thoughts in your mind that you then have to deal with. A further feature of NATs is that they may spring from, and therefore match with, deeper and more absolute beliefs that you hold.

The 'middle layer': assumptions and rules for living

Assumptions link your beliefs to your day-to-day thinking. In this sense, they are the 'middle layer' of your thinking. They also create your 'rules for living'. For example, if you hold a negative belief that you are a boring person, then you may make an assumption that, 'If I talk to people socially, they will find me dull and uninteresting.' Such an *assumption* may activate your *rules for living*. When you receive a party invitation, you may think, 'I won't go. No one will want to talk to me.' Or you may go, but decide, 'I'll just stand by myself in the corner and hope no one notices me. That way, I won't have to talk to people.'

Your rules for living

You may develop a rule for living not to socialize because you consider this will prevent your 'I am boring' belief being put to the test.

Identifying your rules

Can you identify any rules for living of your own? Ask yourself how you cope with those beliefs on a day-to-day basis. For instance, if you believe you are unlovable, one of your rules for living might be to be as nice as pie to everyone at all times, no matter how they treat you, in order to mitigate this.

The 'bottom layer': core beliefs

Such *beliefs* are not event-specific, but are absolute and unchanging. They may have developed from your childhood and/or have been modified or cemented by adult experiences that seem to provide you with 'proof' that these beliefs are true. For example, a partner splitting up with you might serve to confirm an 'I'm unlovable' belief that developed in childhood due to over-critical parents.

The reason we have waited until now to introduce these more deeply-held beliefs is that you will often only discover what these are once you see patterns in your automatic thoughts. For example, you may discover that, when presented with tasks in life that might be challenging, you always find yourself thinking along the lines of, 'I won't be able to do that', 'I'll probably mess this up if I try it' or 'Others find all this far easier than I do'. These thought patterns are giving you information about a possible belief you may hold, which could be, 'I'm inadequate.' This type of belief forms the 'bottom layer' of your thinking. You regard such beliefs as absolute – they are not open to debate, as they are simply (in your mind) facts. You may hold negative beliefs about:

* yourself ('I am worthless')
* others ('People always let you down')
* the world ('Crime is everywhere')
* the future ('Nothing will ever change').

Negative beliefs can be so deep that you rarely consciously notice them. You see them as absolute truths, 'just the way things are', but they are often wrong, or at least obsolete and out of date. Usually stemming from childhood, when you rarely, if ever, question what you learn, they keep you trapped in negativity.

Activation of beliefs causes difficulties

Your beliefs may not be especially consequential unless they are *activated*. For example, someone with a core belief of 'I'm worthless' may be hugely affected if they are turned down for a job. Instead of putting this down to bad luck or heavy competition, their belief will activate assumptions and thoughts about themselves along the lines of, 'I'm probably unemployable', 'I'll probably never get a job', 'Nothing I do works out', etc.

Uncovering beliefs

Uncovering core beliefs isn't necessarily difficult. Sometimes you are only too well aware of the strong views you hold, and sometimes a core belief can simply be expressed as a NAT – you fail in some way and your first thought is, 'I'm hopeless' or 'I'm stupid'. However, to discover those beliefs that tend to lurk outside your consciousness, start by identifying patterns of thinking from your NATs and ask yourself: 'What beliefs do I hold that might make sense of these thought patterns?'

Once you have made a start on this list of beliefs, you can test them by looking back through childhood and early adult experiences for evidence that might make sense of how you came to think that way.

* An 'I'm unlovable' belief might come from being heavily criticized in childhood, or perhaps from one or two disappointing adult relationships that were terminated by the other party.
* Beliefs about others – 'Others cannot be trusted' – might come from past experiences of being let down time and time again.

Rating the strength of your beliefs

Once you have a list of basic beliefs, a vital task is to rate the strength of your belief in them. This is critical *before* you start any work on changing them as you don't want to waste precious time and effort working on beliefs with, say, only a 20 per cent belief rating. Once you have given a subjective rating to each of your negative beliefs (just an approximate figure based on your personal views about the belief), rank them in order of strength of belief, and choose one or two with high belief ratings to work with. You only have so much time and so much energy – don't waste them on the wrong things. You may like to group your beliefs into three categories:

1 Those needing immediate attention (just place one or two here).
2 Those that you might work on in the future.
3 Those that don't, at this moment in time, warrant great effort and attention.

Challenging core beliefs

Don't assume that beliefs are necessarily hard to change. Sometimes the transition can be quite speedy, and may even take place as you challenge your thinking. However, some beliefs are quite rigid and deeply held, and this, in turn, can be why thought challenging is not an especially helpful exercise. No matter how many times you tell yourself that there is a different, more positive way of viewing your thoughts and feelings on a relationship break-up, if these thoughts are quite contrary to an absolute belief that you are worthless, you will not be able to make any progress. In such a case, you will need to work on the belief, rather than the thoughts.

It can also take longer to work on belief change than on thought change. Where you have deeply-held beliefs that have been around for a long time, they will fight you to stay in the frame. Be prepared to work hard if you need to. You may get a pleasant surprise and find the beliefs go quite quickly but if not, that's fine. It simply means you need to work harder for longer, not that they are immovable.

Techniques for changing belief patterns

Changing belief patterns falls into two, linked, categories:
1 Weakening and loosening old beliefs.
2 Strengthening new, more helpful beliefs.

There are many techniques that can help you to achieve this. Try them all – you may find that some work better for you than others.

Weighing up the pros and cons

Ask yourself what the advantages are of hanging on to your old belief. Then ask yourself what are the disadvantages of continuing to hold such beliefs.

Working in this way can help to loosen the idea that your negative belief(s) are helpful and encourage you to look at things with a wider perspective.

Using a continuum

People are often undeservedly hard on themselves with their beliefs. First, select a negative belief. For example, 'I am completely stupid'. Now look at the continuum below:

Someone who cannot read or write				Nobel prize winner
0%_____	25%_____	50%_____	75%_____	100%

Where will you place yourself on the continuum? You will probably place yourself in a far more reasonable position than at the bottom of the scale. Where will you place your work colleague on this list. Your best friend, your uncle, the dustman? As you complete the continuum, reflect on what you find. What does this exercise tell you about the reality of your belief?

Behavioural experiments to test old belief and new belief

You saw earlier how to set up experiments to test the validity of your thoughts. You can use exactly the same skill with your beliefs.

Core belief: I cannot relate to people		
Behavioural experiment	Prediction based on my core belief	What actually happened
Find one thing to say to five different people – for example the person sitting next to me on the bus, the person behind me in the supermarket queue, the receptionist at work, the postman.	They will fail to respond, or may even ignore me.	Everyone responded pleasantly, and three actually engaged me in conversation, although the postman was in a rush.
Revised core belief based on result: I can get on with many people.		

Rephrasing assumptions

In the same way that you found alternative, more balanced thoughts to challenge your NATs, you can do this with your assumptions. For example:

My old beliefs	More balanced alternatives
'If I make mistakes, then I'm a failure.'	'We all make mistakes sometimes; it simply means we are fallible human beings.'
'If this relationship breaks down, then I'll know I'm unlovable.'	'Relationships break down all the time, no matter who we are, and this often says more about the weaknesses of our partner than about us.'

Abandoning inappropriate 'shoulds', 'musts' and 'oughts'

A great many of people's negative, self-defeating thoughts come from using the words 'should', 'must' and 'ought'. These words imply personal failure almost every time you use them. They cause you to make demands on yourself, and suggest that you cannot meet those demands. For example:

* 'I should have good personal relationships.'
* 'I ought to get top marks.'

This is *not* positive thinking. You may believe it is, and that you are motivating yourself by saying these things. In fact, the exact opposite happens. You tend to add an unspoken corollary to your, 'I must …' statement so that it becomes:

* 'I must always be (polite, charming, clever, etc.) and if I am not, then I'm worthless (boring, dreary, not likeable, etc.).'

Your 'shoulds', 'musts' and 'oughts' can extend to your beliefs about others:

* People 'should' be nicer to me.
* Others 'must' consider me when making their plans.

We would like you to visualize gathering up all of these words and dropping them into the nearest rubbish bin. What can you put in their place? One option is using simple acceptance. Adopt the idea that it is acceptable to be fallible and that others also make mistakes.

You can also replace 'shoulds', 'musts' and 'oughts' with softer, less absolute and critical language:

* 'It would be great if I can achieve this, but it's not the end of the world if I don't.'
* 'It would have been better if I'd remembered to ... but I am as fallible as the next person.'

Observation: measuring yourself against others

When you set yourself standards through dysfunctional beliefs – 'I must be perfect at all times or I am a failure', 'I must always be charming and articulate or people will dislike me', 'If I am not kind to others at every opportunity, I am selfish and unlovable' – try observing others around you or consider the behaviour of friends, family and work colleagues. Ask yourself whether they also set themselves these standards.

Creating more helpful beliefs

Weakening negative or inappropriate beliefs is a good start, but you need to develop some alternative, more helpful beliefs to take their place and then work to give these beliefs real strength.

Creating a new belief is one thing, believing in it is another. In the same way that you searched for evidence to support more balanced thinking, you can search for evidence to support core beliefs. You will do this over a longer time frame than checking the validity of NATs, so you may want to keep a record that you can keep updating to increase your confidence and strengthen your belief.

4

additional CBT techniques

We can understand ourselves better by Socratic enquiry – asking ourselves probing 'open' questions, and exploring other ways of looking at situations and problems.

Various techniques can be employed to relieve the physical symptoms that accompany the stress and anxiety associated with problem dwelling. They include breathing techniques, relaxation exercises and distraction methods. A good night's sleep and regular exercise are conducive to general well-being and feeling better about yourself.

Techniques for exploring thoughts and overcoming challenges include imagery and visualization, surveys of your own and other people's thinking and behaviour, video recording to observe your own behaviour, along with simple coping mechanisms and action plans that enable you to come at problems from a fresh angle.

Thinking in more detail, deconstructing negative thoughts, constructing more helpful thinking, and cultivating visual awareness are further techniques that can help in problem-solving.

Action-related strategies can combat those errors in thinking and behaviour that can maintain problems.

More skills to help you

An emphasis on open-questioning techniques

It is interesting how often people have helpful, enquiring conversations with others, but rarely with themselves. 'What's gone wrong?', 'How did that happen?', 'Is it really as bad as all that?', 'Why don't you consider...?', 'Have you thought about...?' These questions come easily when empathizing with someone else's difficulties, yet you rarely use these same skills – for that's what they are – on yourself.

These are the type of open questions – questions that engender a thoughtful and considered answer – that you need to use when trying to understand and resolve any emotional or practical difficulties that you have yourself.

How does it help?

Socratic enquiry – open questioning – encourages you to consider aspects of your difficulties that you might have dismissed. It works on the principle that you have a great deal of valuable information known to you but 'outside your awareness'. That is, you are failing to take the information into account when formulating negative thoughts and beliefs.

Learn to have dialogues with yourself

In a sense, you need to become both Socrates and his student. Simple questions will be very helpful when you review a negatively perceived event. For example:

* How did I feel?
* What went through my mind when I felt that way?
* What was my reaction?
* Have I evidence to support my thoughts?
* What conclusions might I draw from the extra information I now have?

Essentially, you are looking for answers that will encourage you to explore the situation further and possibly revise your current conceptualization (your map) of the problem.

Using Socratic enquiry to challenge beliefs

Beliefs often seem like facts, with little room for manoeuvre. Making some simple enquiries of yourself will help you. For example:

* 'How helpful is it to me, to hold such a belief?'
* 'If this belief is a truth, how do other people deal with it?'
* 'What evidence do I have that this belief is true?'

This sort of enquiry will loosen your unhelpful belief and give you an opportunity to generate alternative, more helpful, possibilities. Ask yourself:

* 'Now that I have considered the bigger situation, how do I view what worried me originally?'
* 'Do I still view my original belief as the worst thing that could happen?'

Socratic questioning is not about 'changing minds'.

Finally, retain the idea that this type of questioning is not necessarily to get you to change your mind about something. It is to allow you to explore all the alternatives and options to thinking, feeling and acting that will encourage you to develop a view of your own, through guided discovery, that may be more hopeful and optimistic than your previous negative thoughts or beliefs.

Relief of physical symptoms

There can be times when you do not feel good at all – when your mood is low or your anxiety high – when your first desire is simply to relieve the immediate physical symptoms of your distress.

There is some argument about the usefulness of symptom relief as a CBT technique.

Many professionals take the view that they don't want your confidence to be placed in a symptom relief element of subsuming your next panic attack. They – quite rightly – want you not to have any more panic attacks.

Some people however feel that they cannot face the challenges of overcoming anxiety, for example, without a little symptom relief help first. It is your choice. If you choose to try symptom relief, there are three main strategies:

1 Deep breathing
2 Relaxation techniques
3 Distraction.

We will look later at relaxation and breathing exercises. Here we look at distraction.

Adjusting your focus

The use of distraction is based on the view that you can only think about one thing at a time. Therefore, focusing on relaxing, pleasant thoughts may prevent your negative worries dominating. However, many people find distracting themselves from their worrying thoughts extremely difficult. Distractions that work best, therefore, are those that require absorption and mental stimulus. This may be something as stimulating as a crossword puzzle, as absorbing as a jigsaw puzzle, or – if you are trapped on a train and have nothing around you – a simple nonsense such as picking a number and counting backwards in 3s or 7s, down to zero. Chatting to someone, with the focus on listening to what they have to say, can work very well. Other forms of distraction, can include listening to music, watching television, reading or counting the number of red cars going by. Develop what works best for you.

Imagery and role play

Imagery as a technique in CBT is a powerful, diverse tool. It is not within the remit of this book to describe imagery techniques because many of them need the guidance of a qualified professional to be effective.

Unless you are working with a therapist, you need a willing partner to assist with role plays. However, role plays can be extremely useful in working through feared or difficult situations – you and your partner can take turns in playing the different parties in the event and testing your actions and reactions in a safe place. Many people find that using this technique gives them great confidence when they face the real thing.

For example, if you have to find the courage to ask your boss for a rise, ask your partner to play the boss while you practise voicing the best way to approach the matter. You can then reverse the role play and play the boss yourself, so that you can see how someone else might deal with them.

Conducting a survey

This is a useful tool for loosening the validity of unhelpful negative thoughts and beliefs. Your survey can be conducted in a variety of ways to test out any number of things. In its simplest form you can survey, say, a dozen friends or work colleagues to ask their views on something that worries you. Do they think that 'only doing your absolute best at all times is acceptable', for example? Do they consider it a heinous fault to make a 'reasonable' attempt at something, rather than always striving for perfection? Why do they see things this way? What is their view on such and such? What might you conclude by finding that many people don't see things as you do, or worry about things as much as you do?

'Ask a friend'

Almost everyone has a tendency to be far harder on themselves than on others. You make allowances for the mistakes of friends and work colleagues; you understand that for others a 'bad step' doesn't make a 'bad person', yet when it comes to yourself, you show no leniency. An excellent tool for rebalancing your views of yourself or your problems is to ask yourself the following questions:

* 'If my best friend was feeling this way, rather than me, what would I say to them?'
* 'What evidence would I point out to my best friend to help them see that their pessimistic thought or negative self-assessment was not 100 per cent true?'

The answer you come up with will usually be quite different to your own negative thinking. People are always much wiser and more constructive at finding positive qualities in others than in themselves. Use your evidence-gathering skills to prove your point, and – almost certainly – show how little evidence there is for the self-defeating thoughts that your 'friend' has.

Developing coping skills

Do not think we are guiding you towards the idea that all negative thoughts are incorrect. On many occasions they are 'spot on'. You are in a jam or a tight spot, things have gone terribly wrong, you have made a huge error and, while trying to see things in a positive light – 'At least nobody died' or 'Thank goodness it wasn't a total disaster' – you need to develop a sense of realism and ability to put together a 'disaster relief' action plan.

Define the worst-case scenario and how you might cope

Asking yourself, 'What is the worst outcome I could predict and, in case, how would I feel and how would I cope?' is a superb question for developing your coping skills. It invites you to name the problem and the emotion, which you can then work on, but, more importantly, it invites you to develop a coping mechanism. You may surprise yourself by considering how rarely you do think about 'managing' when things go very wrong.

Develop an action plan

Don't spend too much time trying to find more positive cognitions. Become action-oriented, and ask yourself:
* 'What can I do – if anything – about this now?'
* 'In what way can I make things better?'
* 'If this cannot be undone, will openness/honesty/apology be beneficial?'
* 'If the worst comes to the worst, how will I cope?'

You will derive great confidence from this.

Think constantly in solution-focused mode, rather than trying to see things differently. Becoming active will help you to cope better emotionally with a difficult problem.

Developing visual awareness

When your mood is low, your focus of attention will be on your negative thinking. We call this *negative cognitive bias* (leaning towards a pessimistic point of view) – not only are you over-focused on pessimistic thoughts; you are also discounting optimistic, positive viewpoints and events.

Open your eyes

One simple tool you can use to correct this is to develop increased visual awareness of what is going on around you. For instance, you may be driving your car from A to B, and ruminating as you go over your difficulties and concerns. What are you missing?

Have you noticed how blue the sky is, the wonderful colours of the trees in autumn, the laughing children playing in the park? Probably not. You will need to practise this, so develop a behavioural experiment that might require you to focus on at least three positive things the next time you go out.

We are not diminishing genuine problems and concerns that need addressing in any way, but practise balancing this with a visual awareness of the joys of life. It may give you a different perspective and raise your mood.

Don't give up

Albert Ellis (1988) is famous for saying (rightly) that one of the main reasons that people don't change – or not as much as they would like to – is that they give up on the hard work and effort required to make positive changes.

Dr Robert Anthony (2004) cites research that shows it takes approximately 21 days (of daily practice) to break an old, destructive habit or form a new, positive habit. Please keep this in mind.

Errors of thought and action

Reducing activity

When your mood is low, you often find that making any sort of effort is, well, an effort. The answer seems obvious. Do little and wait until your low mood passes and you 'feel more like it'. Yet you are trapped in another maintaining behaviour. The less you do, the less confident you feel. If you don't go out, your social skills diminish and your friends give up on you. If you don't try, you lose the pleasurable feelings of stretching yourself and possibly succeeding. If you don't exercise, your body will close down. You then feel physically worse – which confirms your view that you are too tired (or ill) to do much. Your motivation disappears and you are in a vicious circle of maintaining your low mood.

Negative focusing

Hyper-vigilance

If you have a worry – perhaps about developing some sort of serious illness, for example – it might seem natural (a good idea, in fact) to keep extremely vigilant at all times, to ensure you don't miss an early indication that your fears may be about to materialize. The problem with focusing so strongly in this way is that you constantly look for evidence to support your worries.

Selective focus

Imagine you have concerns about your popularity with others. You may focus on every negative nuance of people you are with – noticing if someone doesn't smile at you broadly enough or turns away a little too quickly to speak to someone else. You will quickly give a negative interpretation to this, and you are so busy doing so that you miss the friendly girl sitting next to you, or the drink offered by someone you were speaking with earlier. Your focus is selective and negatively biased – as such, it maintains your problem.

Perfectionism

Where your negative beliefs in yourself are very strong, you may set yourself targets and standards that you feel you must achieve in order to regain self-validation – but which are often unreasonable. Thus, you set yourself up to fail, and the worthlessness belief is maintained, rather than reduced, for example.

Procrastination

Procrastination involves putting things off that you should be facing and dealing with. Negative thinking strategies tend to have a crippling, disempowering effect and the problem with procrastination is that it engenders a sense of helplessness. You start believing that you can't do anything – that it is beyond you – and you fail to trigger problem-solving skills that would move you forward.

Depressive rumination

Rumination involves going over the same old ground again and again without adding any new or positive thinking to it. Perhaps you constantly replay past negative, upsetting or even disastrous events in your mind, turning over the idea that perhaps you could have done something differently or 'If only things hadn't worked out that way.'

One way of breaking this depressive, maintaining cycle is to ask yourself questions such as:

* 'What have I learned from this experience?'
* 'In what way am I now stronger, as a result of this experience?'

While not changing reality in any way, these questions provide access to some sort of positive or learning experience to be gained from past misfortunes.

Is physiology part of CBT?

Yes, definitely. Physiological responsiveness is one of the four interacting systems (with thoughts, moods and behaviour) central to the cognitive behavioural therapy (CBT) model. For this reason it is important for CBT to include the development of skills that relate to improving physiological symptoms.

Sleep difficulties

One of the most common problems when your mood is low and your thoughts negative and ruminative is getting a good night's sleep.

Specific worries, general anxiety and depression can all trigger sleep problems. These difficulties can exacerbate other symptoms – being regularly exhausted makes it harder to fight negative thoughts and feelings.

Overcoming sleep difficulties

Below are some suggestions for tackling your sleep problems.

* Relax before going to bed. Have a warm bath, listen to music, or practise meditation or yoga.
* Write a list of things to be tackled tomorrow. This will relax your brain as it will not have to keep a mental note of what needs to be done.
* Take regular, moderate exercise such as swimming or walking – but leave a three-hour gap before going to bed.
* Cut out evening coffee. Caffeine is a stimulant.
* Alcohol causes sleep disturbance because your body detoxifies it. Reducing your alcohol consumption will have a positive effect on your ability to sleep.
* Don't eat heavy meals close to bedtime.
* If you cannot avoid irregular hours, you can keep your biological clock tuned in by having four hours' sleep at the same time every day.
* Don't lie in bed worrying that you can't sleep. Get up and do something relaxing until you feel sleepy – then go back to bed.

Reducing the physiological symptoms of worry

There are two well-recognized physiological techniques for calming the physical manifestations of worry – deep breathing and muscle relaxation.

Learning to control your breathing is a big step towards controlling the physical sensations of high emotion. Becoming physically calm rests your brain, which prevents your emotional mind from dominating the proceedings. If you learn this simple skill, and practise it regularly, you will be well on the way to feeling calmer.

1 Place your hands on your stomach and chest.

2 Now breathe in slowly through your nose.

3 Ensure as you do this that the hand on your stomach rises, and the hand on your chest remains as still as possible.

4 Now exhale slowly and feel the hand on your stomach gently fall back.

This is a simple breathing technique that you can use whenever you like.

Don't wait for a crisis

One of the weaknesses of skills, such as good breathing, is that people feel they can simply use them in a crisis. However, if you wait for a crisis, you are not going to be skilled enough, or practised enough, to be able to use this tool on an almost unconscious, second-nature basis. Practice regularly, using the 'rule of four'.

* Breathe in and out to a count of four.
* Do this for four minutes.
* Do it four times a day.

Muscle relaxation for calming emotion

The idea behind muscular relaxation is that it will eventually enable you to relax yourself quickly and at will, thus immediately helping to reduce high emotions before they become out of control.

Progressive muscle relaxation involves tensing and relaxing, in succession, 16 different muscle groups of the body working from your hands, up your arms to your head, then steadily down your trunk and legs.

Make sure you are in a setting that is quiet and comfortable and take a few slow, deep breaths before you start. Then tense each muscle group hard for about 10 seconds and let go of it suddenly, enjoying the sensation of limpness. Allow the relaxation to develop for at least 15–20 seconds before going on to the next group of muscles. Notice how the muscle group feels when relaxed, in contrast to how it felt when tensed, before going on to the next group of muscles.

Exercise

When you exercise – by which we mean doing something to raise your heart rate for a period of 30 minutes or so at any one time – your brain naturally manufactures more serotonin. This is the 'feel-good' chemical that helps you to maintain a good mood. This is why you will see, for instance, athletes at the end of a long race, when they should rightfully be exhausted and down on their knees, running extra laps and jumping in the air. The increase in their serotonin is so great that they are quite 'high' at this point.

5

CBT and specific difficulties

CBT can be used to treat depression and anxiety disorders.

Depression is very common. It is curable and can go away of its own accord. People become depressed for many reasons, including biological predisposition and difficult life experiences. Mild depression can be tackled with simple CBT methods, but more severe cases need professional help.

CBT understands depression as a mood disorder caused by your negative thoughts and perceptions. It can be alleviated by tackling the negative thinking bias, by encouraging activities which lift the mood, and by changes in behaviour.

Anxiety manifests in different forms – generalized anxiety disorder (GAD), post-traumatic stress disorder (PTSD), health anxiety, obsessive compulsive disorder (OCD), phobias and panic.

A certain amount of anxiety is healthy as it protects from taking unwarranted risks, but disproportionate levels are unhealthy. The physical symptoms of anxiety can feed back into anxious thoughts, creating an interacting 'anxiety spiral'.

Do you actually have depression?

Not everyone is aware that the way they think and act may be indicative of depression. Some people suffer for many years without having an awareness of the problem. For others, it can hit like a truck and you are in no doubt at all that things have gone horribly wrong emotionally.

There are great variances in the level of depression ranging from mild to extremely severe. In the latter case, sufferers would be wise to seek professional help. However, except in severe cases, people can learn to tackle depression themselves using cognitive behavioural therapy (CBT) skills and techniques.

The causes of depression

There is no one specific cause for depression but rather a variety of possibilities that may come together or be present individually. These causes can include genetics, biological predisposition, certain types of upbringing, and events of adult life that can be either chronic or specific and traumatic. A major culprit of modern-day life is stress, which is one of the most common influences on our state of mind. Depression can be:

* **event-specific.** This type of depression can usually be tracked back to a particular trauma or negative lifestyle change, probably in the fairly recent past.
* **non-specific.** This type of depression seems to have a life of its own, and its appearance (and disappearance) bears little obvious relationship to your circumstances and general lifestyle at any point in time.

Depression is, in simple terms, a mood disorder. This is to say that it is caused not by events (although they may trigger it) but by your thoughts and perceptions about specific events, about yourself, about life in general, and about the future.

Depression is curable, and even in those who seek no treatment and make no attempt to try to get better in any way, it usually goes away of its own accord. However, it is a very distressing illness, and the feelings of bleakness and hopelessness it engenders need not be supported – there is a better way to live.

Negative automatic thoughts again

One of the hallmarks of depression is an extreme negative thinking bias (as always, focusing on worst-case scenarios). Where your mood is low, your thoughts will also be extremely negative and you will find it hard to motivate yourself. This will lead to a cycle of inactivity which, in turn, will increase your depression.

Breaking the cycle will break the hold of the depression. As you will notice, there is a cognitive element, a behavioural element and a physiological element to the cycle, and you will be able to use your CBT tools to make changes to any and all of these areas to lift your mood.

The cognitive component: getting your rational mind back on track

In order to break this spiral of negativity, you need your rational mind to work a little harder. This means starting to challenge the negative outlook that has crept in as a default. Because negative thoughts are particularly severe in depression, you will need to use 'Where's the evidence?' strongly, starting out with the evidence you have to support your negative thinking before moving on to evidence that might support an alternative way of looking at things.

Shifting beliefs before changing thoughts

Although this alternative thought makes good sense as a rational response where the belief is 'I am weak and useless', believing such a positive option is going to be almost impossible. However, if the belief can, at first, be shifted from 'I'm weak and useless' to 'I can occasionally stand my ground', then the balanced thought becomes a believable possibility.

The physiological component: get active

Depression saps your energy. It can leave you feeling tired and exhausted, even at the start of the day, leading to inactivity. This in turn keeps your mood low.

Depression can sap your motivation and desire to do anything. Because it leaves you feeling flat and uninterested in normal activities, the tendency is not to do them. Staying at home feels so much easier and safer. However, as you will appreciate, 'The less we do, the less we want to do' state of mind operates with a vengeance with depression.

Activity scheduling

A basic CBT tool in dealing with inactivity in depression, and its negative repercussions, is an 'Activity Schedule'. Activity Schedules serve two clear purposes:

1 They encourage you to structure your day and build a little more activity into it.
2 They identify patterns for your moods. You can record when your mood is at its lowest, and you will be able to see what levels and types of activity or inactivity exacerbate your low mood, and when you feel somewhat better.

An activity schedule should look something like this:

Time	MON	TUES	WED	THURS	FRI	SAT	SUN
7 a.m.	Get up, shower, etc.	Get up, shower, etc.	Get up, shower, etc.	Get up, shower, etc.	Get up, shower, etc.	Sleep	Sleep
8 a.m.	Breakfast	Go to gym	Breakfast	Go to dentist	Walk dog	Sleep	Sleep

And so on, through the day. You would then place a red asterisk against the times and situations when you feel at your lowest and a green asterisk against the times you feel at your best. There should be patterns in when you feel good and when you feel low. These patterns should tell you something.

Regular exercise provides your brain with a natural boost of serotonin – the brain chemical that provides the 'feel-good' factor that we have in abundance when our mood is optimistic and positive. Physical exercise is one of the best mood lifters around.

What causes anxiety?

Anxiety is one of the most distressing emotions you can feel, in part because the physiology is so severe – heart-pounding, stomach churning, shaking, dizziness and a variety of other symptoms give you further cause to worry. Anxiety is caused by the belief that situations are more frightening than they really are. The physical symptoms of anxiety play a great part in this over-estimation of the perceived threat, as they are seen themselves as significant indicators that something is seriously wrong.

Anxiety as a good thing

Anxiety isn't always a bad thing. Aaron Beck (1976) refers to 'nature favouring anxious genes'. Anxiety prevents you from walking in front of buses or falling over cliffs. It keeps you safe. Albert Ellis (1979) refers to the concept of 'healthy and unhealthy anxiety'. In essence, anxiety is only a problem to you if it is inappropriate to the circumstances you find yourself in. In this chapter, we look at inappropriate anxiety.

Whereas in depression your focus is usually on past and present events that disturb you, anxiety causes you to worry about events that have not – and may not – happen. Sir Winston Churchill told a story of visiting a man on his deathbed who told him, 'I have had a great many worries and troubles in my life, most of which have never happened.'

Normalizing the physiology

Feelings that you describe as 'anxiety' or 'tension' are simply the result of a normal bodily reaction to danger or threat in the world about you. This bodily reaction, called 'automatic arousal', helped prepare the cave people to muster the physiological resources to either fight or run away when faced with danger along the lines of sabre-toothed tigers and such like. Be assured that when you have these feelings, your body is simply trying to *help* you – not to cause you any distress.

When you face danger, messages pass from your brain to different parts of the body, telling it to speed up and be prepared for extra activity. You may experience similar sensations when you take vigorous exercise, and many of the physical reactions in anxiety are like those after, say, running around the block – heart beating fast, face flushing and legs feeling like jelly.

How anxiety develops: the anxiety spiral

Physical sensations that occur when you are confronted with an anxiety-provoking situation can often aggravate it. These symptoms may be anticipatory or they may be evoked by the memory of a past experience when you became anxious. Feeling that something is physically wrong can increase the tension and exacerbate the symptoms. The result can be seen in an 'anxiety spiral', or a vicious cycle of anxiety. Panic can ensue, as can the desire to run away or avoid the situation.

Think about a recent situation you have found stressful and whether your reaction was similar to that in the anxiety spiral.

Factors that maintain anxiety

Safety behaviours

Safety behaviours, as the name implies, are tactics you embrace in order – you believe – to keep you safe from threat or harm. For example, someone who fears having a panic attack in the supermarket simply never shops in one. Someone who fears being found dull and uninteresting never accepts social invitations.

If you think you might fail at something, then don't even try it. These seem like obvious, natural solutions to your fears and worries – and, what is more, they seem to work. However, on the down side, they cause your worries to stay with you as you never give yourself the opportunity to discover that the perceived threat was either invalid or manageable.

Avoidance

Avoidance is the most common safety behaviour of all, and one that many people use occasionally. As we have described above, simply failing to place yourself in situations of perceived threat appears to keep you safe. Yet its downfall is that it fails to allow you to discover that the threat was either non-existent or manageable, and thus avoidance becomes a *problem-maintaining* behaviour.

Escape

Escape is a first cousin of avoidance. It means that you tolerate situations until you feel the physical and/or emotional sensations that worry you – then you make a quick getaway.

Escape is often planned in advance – emergency forward planning. You sit next to the emergency exit at the school play, or only accept an aisle seat in the cinema. You put yourself in a position to abscond quickly if you feel that you need to. A consequence of this is that you not only fail to discover whether the threat is real or if you might cope with it if it is – you give the perceived threat more credence than it deserves, which again maintains its hold over you.

Overcoming anxiety

Cognitive strategies

The key error that anxious people make is that they focus on ways to *reduce their anxious feelings* by using safety behaviours. Instead, they need to focus on *reducing the strength of the erroneous belief* that drives the anxiety. As the belief strength diminishes, so will the anxiety, of its own accord and permanently.

Challenging your anxious thoughts

A Thought Record can help to re-evaluate the severity and/or likelihood of the threat causing anxiety. The accuracy of predictions can be evaluated by assessing outcomes.

* What did I think would happen?
* What actually happened?
* What can I learn from that?

Theory A versus Theory B

This is an excellent technique, used especially with cases of irrational worry, such as those seen in obsessive compulsive disorder (OCD), developed by Salkovskis and Kirk (1997). This theory invites the anxious person to consider two alternative propositions. The first (Theory A) is that his or her fears are correct and that the problem is therefore one of catastrophe. For example, 'If I travel in a lift, I will have a panic attack that will cause me heart failure.' The second (Theory B) is that the problem is possibly not one of catastrophe, but one of worry about catastrophe. For example, 'I worry that I might panic, and that this might cause me to be ill.' You can then test these alternative theories using various CBT skills – looking for evidence, testing beliefs, weighing up the pros and cons of likelihood, and so on.

Imaginal exposure

Imaginal exposure is used in the treatment of certain anxiety disorders where the fear of testing out the negative predictions is too great. Instead, you start by simply imagining yourself, for example, as an agoraphobic, opening the front door and going outside.

Behavioural strategies

Devising experiments to test out the validity of catastrophic predictions – in principle, learning to 'face your fears' – is invaluable for tackling avoidance head on. Develop an action plan for graded exposure, where going 'cold turkey' would be too traumatic.

Physiological strategies

Learning to reduce the physical sensations of anxiety through relaxation and deep breathing is extremely useful when the consequences of high anxiety severely impair performance or the ability to face a feared situation.

What is meant by 'anxiety disorders'?

In a therapeutic sense, the term 'anxiety disorders' covers a number of psychological problems including GAD (generalized anxiety disorder), phobias, panic, health anxiety, social anxiety, agoraphobia, post-traumatic stress disorder and obsessive compulsive spectrum disorders.

Generalized anxiety disorder

'Generalized anxiety disorder' (GAD) is a term used to describe symptoms of intense anxiety (worrying, tension, impairment) without the anxiety being focused on a specific area (for instance, on health, social situations or phobias). As with all anxiety disorders, GAD is characterized by excessive worry and anxiety that persists over a reasonably long period of time. This chronic anxiety state is difficult to control, causes distress and limits a person's activities.

GAD sufferers usually find that as one worry resolves itself, another comes along and takes its place. In other words, it is not the events that are the problem, but the sufferer's consistent perception of events as threats and problems.

The best way to defeat generalized worry involves breaking this cycle by understanding it, and then eliminating it by addressing the underlying fears. This can be achieved by the following.
* **Identifying and challenging unhelpful thoughts.**
* **Learning to live with uncertainty.**
* **Overcoming avoidance** and learning to face the fear that the worry represents.
* **Using strategies such as distraction** when worries flood in.

Phobias

A phobia is a form of anxiety that has a specific focus. For example, a fear of spiders, or of being in open spaces or of heights.

The usual treatment for a phobia is graded exposure and desensitization to the fear. Where the phobic fear is strong you can start with imaginal exposure to the feared situation. Once you are comfortable with this, move on to the next stage.

Panic

Panic is extreme anxiety where the physical symptoms become so marked and frightening that the person misinterprets these sensations and believes some harm is going to come to them, or that they are going to lose control completely.

Panic can start from a small, indiscriminate trigger – perhaps a missed heartbeat or a momentary breathing difficulty. The anxiety is initially created by a misinterpretation of what that small trigger means.

Avoidance and escape are the usual ways of dealing with panic. Once out of the feared situation, the individual calms down. While this causes a temporary reduction in panic symptoms, the person does not learn that had they not fled the scene but stood their ground and waited out the panic attack, nothing would have happened and the attack would simply have died away.

Overcoming panic involves challenging the negative predictions and looking at less threatening alternative explanations for the marked physical sensations. For example, this would mean recognizing that the sensations are due to anxiety, which is not harmful, rather than to impending heart failure, which is.

Health anxiety

In the case of health anxiety, you make the assumption that, because you have pain or another physical symptom then you must have a serious health complaint. Even when health is checked, tests are carried out by doctors and specialists, and the individual has been assured that nothing is medically wrong with them, they are still not reassured and a preoccupation with health problems persists.

As with other types of anxiety, it is the interpretation of the worrying thoughts that needs to be identified.

You can test your fears and beliefs by various methods. One is to investigate the evidence and ask yourself, 'What evidence is there that I have a serious health problem or disease?'

Social anxiety

'Social anxiety' is a term used to describe feeling extreme anxiety and discomfort in social situations. There is a fear of being judged harshly by other people, behaving in an inappropriate or embarrassing way, or being humiliatingly publicly exposed. The person may not actually do anything that is embarrassing but they feel that they have done so, or fear that if they do expose themselves to the scrutiny of others, humiliation and disaster will follow. Research shows that social anxiety affects both men and women equally. It often begins in adolescence and in its early stages it will show as extreme shyness.

Post-traumatic stress disorder

Post-traumatic stress is an anxiety-related condition caused by an adverse reaction to a traumatic or extremely stressful event. Many different kinds of events can lead to post-traumatic stress disorder (PTSD), including being a victim of crime or abuse (physical or sexual) or being involved in a serious accident. People who work in high-risk safety professions, such as soldiers or fire officers, may experience PTSD as they are more likely to witness traumatic events or to experience personal danger or injury.

Because of the nature of the treatment of PTSD, professional help would normally be the best way forward for overcoming this anxiety problem.

Obsessive compulsive disorder

Obsessive compulsive disorder (OCD) is the most commonly known of the OCD spectrum disorders, which include body dysmorphic disorder (feelings of revulsion about physical appearance), obsessive behaviours such as trichotillomania (where the sufferer constantly pulls their hair out) and Tourette's syndrome (where the sufferer has involuntary tics and twitches and occasionally shouts out nonsense).

An essential difference between OCD and other anxiety disorders lies in the irrational content of the negative predictions made. The individual also usually appreciates this – 'I know it's all nonsense', 'I know this couldn't possibly really happen' – but nonetheless, once the anxious thoughts take hold, the desire to reduce the anxiety by any means becomes paramount and overtakes rationality.

There are many techniques for getting over OCD, but still the most widely regarded is the behavioural technique of exposure and response prevention. This requires the sufferer to expose themselves to the irrational fear (in a structured and graded way) and to resist engaging in the usual ritualistic safety behaviour. Professional guidance may be needed to overcome OCD.

CBT for developing strengths

Low self-esteem can be made worse by your perception of what goes on around you and your sense of your abilities to cope. CBT can help by challenging negative thoughts, and by exploring over-personalization and self-pity.

Perfectionism is a recipe for failure, as there is no such thing as 'perfect', other than the meaning you attribute to it in your own thinking. It can be combatted by mapping thoughts, then weighing up alternative views.

Resilience helps you cope with stress, adversity, loss or trauma. Building resilience involves becoming more self-aware and open to accepting help from others when it is needed.

Assertive behaviour is about clear communication, even in stressful situations, without recourse to ridicule, or becoming unduly aggressive.

While anger can be a useful motivational tool, inappropriate anger can be destructive. Recognising that it is a problem is the first step, and there are techniques which can help to control it. In extreme cases, professional help may be needed.

Low self-esteem

Do you feel that you suffer from low self-esteem?

Low self-esteem can be traced back to a variety of factors, most probably your upbringing, when you may have been heavily criticized and given little confidence in yourself. Perhaps you were bullied at school or found it hard to fit in. It may also have been caused by events in adulthood that have made you revise your view of yourself, for example, being fired from your job or a relationship break-up.

How you perceive what goes on around you and how you interpret your abilities to deal with things has a great impact on self-esteem.

One of the key features of low self-esteem is that you crave approval from others. But you cannot rely on this. The moment you say, 'If he had not done that, I would not have felt this way', 'I only acted that way because of the way she behaved', you remain trapped in your view that others are responsible for how you feel and what you do.

You risk suffering from low self-esteem forever when you blame others for making you feel the way that you do. You may be right but it is not about what other people do, it is about how you respond to what they do that decides how you feel about yourself.

Once you realize that no one else has control over how you feel and that you have excellent control over how you feel, you can put the lid on negative emotions.

When you over-personalize, you erroneously feel that you are to blame for the perceived negative reactions of others. 'If someone disagrees with me, then I must be wrong, and that makes me stupid.' These types of thoughts will maintain your low self-esteem.

You need to identify these thoughts and counteract them. Here are some suggestions for broadening your thinking skills to prevent over-personalization:

* Have respect for the opinions of others in the same way that you hope they will respect yours.
* Distinguish between opinion and fact.

* Have confidence in your own views.
* Others have their own problems.
* Other people don't always react in the best possible way.

Every time you run yourself down by letting negative thoughts about yourself dominate your mind, you are indulging in self-pity. Self-pity is similar to being locked into victim mode, except that on this occasion you are not blaming others as much as you are blaming yourself.

Bringing positive qualities into focus

When you have self-critical thoughts, instead of simply accepting them, challenge them, look for alternatives and create a more balanced view of yourself. You will almost certainly find that you are discounting a lot of positive points about yourself and acknowledging them will help to raise your self-esteem.

Positive Event Log

Another 'self-esteem lifter' can be to keep a daily 'Positive Event Log'. Each evening, take a moment to write down three positive things that happened during the day. These can be big ('I got a promotion at work') or small ('The milkman said hello'). They all have equal value. Next, write down why you think these positive things happened. For example, 'I got a promotion at work because my employer considers me to be good at my job' or 'The milkman smiled at me because he sees me as a friendly person'. Don't worry that your answers are sometimes subjective viewpoints – simply write down what you think.

Improving your self-esteem is essential to developing other life skills. Once you feel at ease with yourself, you will have the confidence to tackle more and you will not be too disturbed by risk of failure.

What is perfectionism?

Many people's negative views of themselves are driven by unhelpful thinking about the standards they should be able to reach in order to feel good about themselves. These are often bright and intelligent people, doing well in their lives, but they are not reaching the 'perfect way of being' that they believe they should attain.

Perfectionism has become the bane of modern life. In our competitive, ultra-fast lifestyles, we find ourselves feeling dissatisfied and upset when we fail to achieve the ultimate in 'just so-ness'. You drive yourself to be the perfect home-maker, cook, parent or property magnate – and feel a failure if you aren't. It is much healthier (but, it seems, increasingly harder) to accept your imperfections, cut yourself some slack, and simply relax.

Perfectionism can mean setting yourself up for failure

This is because it is almost impossible to achieve a perfect score. In many cases, it is impossible to know what that score would be.

In aiming for perfection, you will almost certainly fail every time.

Perfectionism as a psychological problem has increased in proportion to the increased activity in people's lives generally. Many people work hard to achieve a great deal in a limited time, and this puts pressure on them to achieve more with less. Working life especially can be very competitive, and the desire to succeed, to be measured positively, to be liked and respected has moved, within the minds of many, from a preference to a highly pursued desire – something to be achieved at any cost.

Experience shows that the trait usually develops in childhood, often from parents, teachers or contemporaries who drive a child to constantly do better – 80 per cent should be 90 per cent; 90 per cent should be 100 per cent. Being in the football team wasn't good enough unless you were captain. Playing an instrument required you to practise relentlessly, and then some more. The legacy for many young people is they feel that, no matter what they do, it is never good enough. You may carry this 'Nothing I do is ever good enough' belief with you into adulthood as a self-defeating belief.

Perfectionist views can be challenged by looking at their advantages and disadvantages compared to alternative views, and by comparing them with the attitudes of other people.

Perfectionist thinking dictates that satisfaction from doing something is based on how effectively you performed. You can test out whether this is actually true by focusing on some of the tasks you have to do and treating them like behavioural experiments. Look for evidence of satisfaction, and rate it.

This will help you to loosen the belief you may have that the only way to feel good is to do things perfectly.

The importance of resilience

Resilience can provide protection against emotional disorders, such as depression and anxiety, and can help people to deal constructively with the after-effects of trauma. Learning how to become resilient – having the ability to stand firm in the face of adversity and to respond strongly to emotions that might be upsetting or difficult to deal with – has in recent years been signposted as an important developmental characteristic.

How resilient are you now?

People with resilience harness inner strengths and tend to recover more quickly from a setback or challenge – whether this is a job loss, an illness or the death of a loved one. In contrast, people who are less resilient may dwell on problems, feel victimized, become overwhelmed and turn to unhealthy coping mechanisms such as drink or drugs. They may be more likely to develop mental health problems. While resilience won't necessarily make your problems go away, it will give you the ability to see past them, find some enjoyment in life and handle things better.

Resilience is not a personal attribute as this would imply a fixed and unchanging strength that some people have and some do not. It is a more complex process involving both internal cognitive and personality factors and external protective factors. Resilience is also a normal, understandable process. It arises from normal, human qualities such as the ability to rationally solve problems, the capacity to regulate emotion and the ability to form close, supportive ties with others. It is only when these systems are damaged or overwhelmed that natural resilience fails. In other words, it goes hand in hand with being emotionally intelligent. By developing one, you develop the other.

Most importantly, developing resilience means stepping outside of your comfort zone. It means being willing to try a little harder, carry on when you might previously have given up, and feel emotions such as anxiety and fear and yet not back down.

CBT skills to help you improve your resilience include: thought-challenging skills to help you put an optimistic slant on things; taking action step by step; the use of encouraging, positive 'self-talk'; placing things into a larger perspective; and focusing on solutions as opposed to ruminating over problems.

Assertiveness skills

Many people find their perceived inability to behave assertively blocks them from being able to develop self-confidence. Where your fear of confrontation is so high that you avoid it constantly, you are maintaining the problem.

Assertiveness is simply remaining calm, but firm, under pressure.

Lack of assertiveness often goes hand in hand with low self-esteem and feelings of inadequacy. CBT skills can help to overcome this.

When dealing with difficult situations, you can make the mistake of gearing your behaviour to your dominant emotions at the time – rather than to the outcome you wish to achieve. When you behave assertively, you focus on outcomes and results rather than emotions.

Before you can behave assertively, you need to *think* assertively.

Thinking assertively is important since it starts off the train of situation–emotions–behaviour–outcome, and is a point at which you can maintain control and get the situation to work in your favour, rather than against you.

When we behave assertively we ensure that our own needs are met, while also respecting the rights and needs of others.

Take the three-step approach:

* Acknowledge the other person's point of view.
* State your own position.
* Offer a solution.

Learning to be assertive with yourself is as important as learning to be assertive with others. Simply take your assertive thinking skills and apply them to yourself. You have the right to behave however you wish, as long as you take responsibility for it. Most of us sometimes find our fridges full of food beyond its 'sell by' date, have messy drawers we never sort out, tell white lies when turning down boring invitations, fail to tidy up the kitchen for days on end, don't ring our mothers enough, or keep the money we found on the pavement, etc. That's fine. It's normal. You are behaving just like everybody else. Constantly recognize and remember not to beat yourself up for what is really very normal, 'everybody does it' behaviour.

The learning of assertiveness skills is beneficial to anyone who would like to improve their powers of communication.

Controlling anger

One of the hardest emotions to control is anger. For many, no matter how many books they read and seminars they attend on the subject, when push comes to shove, the moment they find themselves riled, emotions take over and they 'lose it'.

Becoming angry doesn't make you a bad person – but it does mean that there are a great many situations you are unnecessarily on the losing end of. If you find yourself getting angry, quite quickly, a lot of the time, you have a problem and need to deal with it.

High anger can ruin both personal and professional relationships, as well as be detrimental to your health. At its worst, anger can also kill. Road rage is an example.

Many believe that tolerance is decreasing and that rage, expressed both verbally and physically, is increasing. Public areas, including hospital wards, libraries, even post offices, all now have written warnings regarding uncontrolled behaviour leading to possible attacks on staff.

People are more concerned than ever with their rights (fuelled, often, by a compensation culture). They are less philosophical, less inclined to 'put things down to experience'. If their demands are not met now in a way that they have come to expect, they become angry.

Suppressing anger

Expressing anger is becoming less and less acceptable, especially in the workplace. This means that by expressing anger inappropriately you may risk losing your job, or at least some disciplinary action. You therefore often bottle anger up, instead of dealing with it, and this can be exceedingly harmful to both your emotional and physical well-being.

Anger is not always a bad thing. The key is being able to control your anger, and to use it only when it is appropriate, while containing it when it is not.

Anger is an appropriate response to some situations; it can provide the motivation to get difficult jobs done, and releasing it can be better than letting it fester.

Healthy anger can let you know that something is wrong. You can use this alert to work out what is worrying you, and then do something positive to change it. For example, if you find yourself becoming irritated every time you need to meet with a particular work colleague, ask yourself why they annoy you so. It may be that they are always late for your meetings, always dominate the discussion, regularly cancel at the last minute, etc. Becoming aware of your anger in these circumstances encourages you to change the situation so that it is less stressful.

Where anger comes from

Anger is built on your expectations regarding the ideals and behaviours of others. You expect people to treat you fairly and they don't. You expect them to be nice to you and they aren't. You expect them to help you and they walk away.

Each time someone breaks a rule of yours, violates a contract or acts against your wishes, a possible option is to react with anger. You do not absolutely have to – it is your choice.

Unfortunately, people do not always feel that they are in control of this choice – you feel unable to manage your emotions and it is as though it has already been decided for you, and you act accordingly.

Learning to own your anger

One of the difficulties of managing anger in difficult situations is the idea that none of this is your fault. If the other person had not done this, that or the other, you would never have reacted in that way. You may be partially right. Someone may have been extremely thoughtless, acted stupidly or whatever, and you may be the victim of their rotten judgement. However, while the other person is responsible for their actions, you are responsible for your response.

Reducing angry emotions with humour

Using humour is an excellent tool for defusing anger. It can help you gain a more balanced perspective and see the funny side. For example, if you have spent the entire afternoon putting together a flat-pack bookcase and, as you stand back to admire it, it falls apart, you can either get furious or laugh. Try laughter. This will take a lot of the edge off your fury, and humour can always be relied on to help relax a tense situation.

If you feel that your anger is really out of control, if it is having an impact on your relationships and on important parts of your life, you might consider professional help to learn how to handle it better. As well as the option of one-to-one therapy, anger management courses are available – learning to manage anger is something many people wish to undertake.

Conclusion

Worries regarding possible setbacks

CBT is highly regarded for its efficacy as a therapy where setbacks are rare. This is because it is an evidence-based teaching model and educates you to become your own therapist, thus giving you instant access to the skills of the model at any time in the future.

Developing confidence in your ability to cope with setbacks can in fact be dependent on actually going through a setback – this is regarded as part of therapeutic practice.

You now have more understanding of the possible causes of setbacks, some of which you can address yourself ahead of time.

You now have the confidence to believe that you will be able to deal with a setback quite effectively if it were to happen, and that it will not in any way be 'going back to the beginning again'.

When to consider professional help

Consider the circumstances in which you might contemplate professional help, and how your thoughts and emotions can play a part in helping you to decide.

There are different therapy options – via the UK NHS, via private insurance – where it might be recommended that you attend a private clinic or hospital that would give you the opportunity of group CBT, either additionally or as an alternative, if you wished it – or self-funding.

If you decide to self-fund, look at the choices this gives you and use them wisely.

You now know what to expect from a timed therapy structure, and that the course of therapy is regularly assessed and reviewed by you and your therapist together.

You can make an informed decision on whether medication might be helpful as a further option.